HEROES OF HISTORY

WILLIAM BRADFORD

Plymouth's Rock

HEROES OF HISTORY

WILLIAM BRADFORD

Plymouth's Rock

JANET & GEOFF BENGE

Emerald
Books

P.O. BOX 635, LYNNWOOD, WA 98046

Emerald Books are distributed through YWAM Publishing. For a full list of titles, including other great biographies, visit our website at www.emeraldbooks.com.

William Bradford: Plymouth's Rock
Copyright © 2016 by Janet and Geoff Benge

Published by Emerald Books
P.O. Box 635
Lynnwood, WA 98046

Library of Congress Cataloging-in-Publication Data

Names: Benge, Janet, 1958– | Benge, Geoff, 1954–
Title: William Bradford : Plymouth's rock / Janet and Geoff Benge.
Description: Lynnwood, Washington : Emerald Books, 2016. | Includes bibliographical references.
Identifiers: LCCN 2016010532 (print) | LCCN 2016011253 (ebook) | ISBN 9781624860928 (paperback) | ISBN 9781624861178 (ebook)
Subjects: LCSH: Bradford, William, 1590–1657—Juvenile literature. | Pilgrims (New Plymouth Colony)—Biography—Juvenile literature. | Separatists—Massachusetts—Biography—Juvenile literature. | Governors—Massachusetts—Biography—Juvenile literature. | Massachusetts—History—New Plymouth, 1620-1691—Juvenile literature. | Massachusetts—Biography—Juvenile literature.
Classification: LCC F68.B8235 B46 2016 (print) | LCC F68.B8235 (ebook) | DDC 974.402092—dc23
LC record available at http://lccn.loc.gov/2016010532

Scripture quotations in this book are taken from the Geneva Bible, 1599 Edition. Published by Tolle Lege Press. All rights reserved.

First printing 2016

Printed in the United States of America

HEROES OF HISTORY

Abraham Lincoln
Alan Shepard
Ben Carson
Benjamin Franklin
Billy Graham
Christopher Columbus
Clara Barton
Davy Crockett
Daniel Boone
Douglas MacArthur
Elizabeth Fry
George Washington
George Washington Carver
Harriet Tubman
John Adams
John Smith
Laura Ingalls Wilder
Louis Zamperini
Meriwether Lewis
Milton Hershey
Orville Wright
Ronald Reagan
Theodore Roosevelt
Thomas Edison
William Bradford
William Penn
William Wilberforce

Available in paperback, e-book, and audiobook formats.
Unit Study Curriculum Guides are available for each biography.
www.emeraldbooks.com

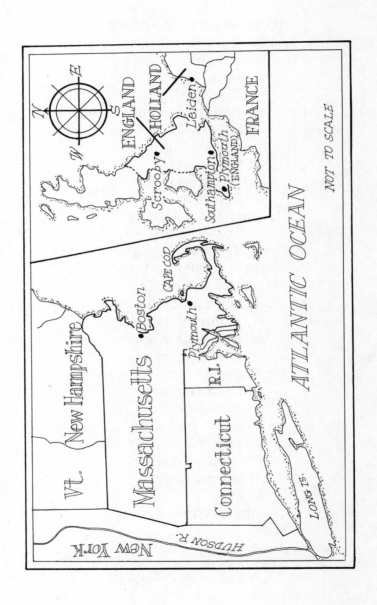

Contents

Chapter 1

Beyond His Imagination

Indians! Indians!" the sentinel yelled as he leaped over the barricade and took cover, a volley of arrows following him. William Bradford grabbed his musket and sprang into action. He could see Myles Standish already crouched at the barricade reloading his gun. Several of the other men fired as William raised his musket to his shoulder and took aim. "We need to get to our muskets," he heard someone yell. "Some of us have already stowed them in the shallop." William turned to see five men running for the boat, trying to avoid the onslaught of arrows. The Indians attempted to cut them off, but Myles rushed out with his cutlass drawn and fended them off.

Having reached the shallop, the men grabbed their guns and dived for cover behind the boat and then opened fire. The arrows kept coming as the

Indians advanced from among the trees. By now William had reloaded and fired again. As more and more muskets fired, the Indians began to fall back. One Indian stood by a pine tree and shot arrow after arrow at the men. The musket balls careening around him did not deter him. William watched as Myles took careful aim and fired. A lead musket ball smashed into the tree trunk right beside the Indian's head, showering the man with shredded bark. Suddenly he turned and ran into the trees. The remaining Indians followed him. The attack was over.

William was shaking as the men quickly gathered up their things and raced to the boat. The men pushed the shallop into the sea and jumped aboard. Soon the sail was up and the boat was leaving the beach behind.

William's shaking turned to shivering, and his teeth chattered. Out on the water it was bone-chillingly cold. He could no longer feel his toes, and the spray splashing over the side of the shallop left a glaze of ice on his jacket. If the cold kept up much longer, William feared that the weather might accomplish what the Indians had tried to do—kill them all.

Before setting out for the New World, William knew that things would be challenging, but what they'd endured so far was beyond his imagination. A month had passed since they dropped anchor off Cape Cod, and they were still no closer to finding a suitable site for their colony. It wasn't supposed to be like this. In fact, they weren't even supposed to be on Cape Cod but should have been farther south, near the mouth of the Hudson River. Unfavorable winds and currents had brought them to this place. With winter descending, they needed to find a home, a place to establish the community William and many others had dreamed about and planned for so long. It wasn't the first time he'd gone to another country in pursuit of his religious freedom, but for William this was certainly the most challenging.

Chapter 2

"Come Out from among Them"

William Bradford set down his quill and stared out the farmhouse window. It was a beautiful summer day, and he could hear the swish of scythes as workers cut wheat in the nearby field. If things had gone differently, William would have been working alongside them, but he was considered too frail to join in the cycles of plowing, planting, and harvesting that went on in the fields around his home at Austerfield in Yorkshire.

No one was quite sure what caused the intense stomach cramps and headaches William experienced. He'd heard his uncles suggest that his condition was related to the many losses he'd suffered in his twelve years of life. William's father, whom he was named after, had died when William was a year old. When William was four years old, his mother married Robert Briggs. William and his older sister, Alice, were sent to live with their grandfather, but he also died, and the two children were sent back to live with their mother, stepfather, and new half brother, Robert. But baby Robert died soon after they arrived.

When William was seven years old, his mother gave birth to another baby, this time a girl named Agnes. Sadly, William's mother died not long after Agnes was born, leaving three children behind. Agnes stayed with her father. Seven-year-old William and ten-year-old Alice, now orphans, went to live on the farm with two of their father's brothers, Thomas and Richard Bradford.

In fact, the farm, plus several other pieces of land around the area, actually belonged to William, or would when he turned twenty-one years of age. As the oldest son, William's father had inherited the farm and the land, which now were being held in trust awaiting William's coming of age and taking direct ownership. This made it difficult for his two uncles to tell him what to do. So when, after arriving to live with them, William began suffering from terrible headaches and stomach cramps, his uncles did not force him outside to work on the farm. Instead, they sent him to a tutor to spend his days learning.

William was a good student and soon mastered reading, writing, and arithmetic. Most of all, he enjoyed reading, and in particular one book his tutor loaned him, *Foxe's Book of Martyrs*. As he sat staring out the farmhouse window, William felt confused. Although he was supposed to be studying Latin, he couldn't get his mind off *Foxe's Book of*

Martyrs. The book, first published in 1563, covered in detail the deaths of many Christian martyrs down through church history. It even dealt with the reign of King Henry VIII, during whose life a dispute with the Roman Catholic Church and the pope led to the separation of the English church from Rome and the establishment of the Church of England. The final chapter of the book was all about the reign of Queen Mary and the bloody struggle to return England to Catholicism. The stories of the deaths of so many devout Christians during this final chapter of the book disturbed William.

From reading the pages of *Foxe's Book of Martyrs*, William learned that the Catholic church, led by the pope, cared most about gaining and keeping political power. Seventy-five years earlier, when King Henry VIII of England had wanted to divorce his wife, Catherine of Aragon, to marry his new love interest, Anne Boleyn, the pope refused to allow it. In response, the king declared that the pope no longer had authority over him or his country and that he would establish a church over which he, not the pope, was the leader. In so doing, King Henry would decide what to do with the taxes and tithes collected by the church. The king quickly took possession of all the land belonging to the Catholic church, which amounted to about one-quarter of England. King Henry VIII stripped Catholic bishops of their power and beheaded those who objected to his actions. It had been quite a bloodbath trying to get the faithful Roman Catholics of England to give up allegiance to their church and the pope and accept the new Church of England.

When King Henry VIII died in 1547, his nine-year-old son, Edward VI, became king in his father's place. Edward had been raised in the Church of England and looked forward to making more reforms, but he died before turning sixteen. On his deathbed, young King Edward insisted that his cousin, Lady Jane Grey, succeed him on the throne. Nine days after she was named the new monarch of England, Henry VIII's oldest daughter, Mary, pressured the government into acknowledging her as the rightful Queen of England, sending the new Queen Jane to the Tower of London, where she was executed several months later for high treason.

Queen Mary of England was a devout Catholic and insisted that the people of England forget the Church of England and return to obeying the pope and the rules of the Catholic church. Once more England was plunged into religious upheaval. Queen Mary soon became known as Bloody Mary, as she ordered the execution of anyone who opposed turning England back into a Catholic country. Among her victims was Thomas Cranmer, the Anglican archbishop of Canterbury, whom she ordered burned at the stake. Hundreds more martyrdoms followed in the wake of her reign of terror.

In 1558, after just five years on the throne, Queen Mary died, and her half sister Elizabeth ascended to the throne. Like her father, Queen Elizabeth staunchly supported the Church of England. Once again Catholicism was outlawed in the country, and the Church of England, with Queen Elizabeth as its leader, became the official church.

It was no wonder, William concluded, that *Foxe's Book of Martyrs* was so gory. Every time a change of monarchy occurred, there were uprisings, beheadings, and burnings at the stake over religious beliefs.

Now, in early 1602, Queen Elizabeth had been ruling England for over forty years, and things in the country were quite stable. The queen seemed mildly tolerant of a group that had sprung up within the Church of England. The members of the group were called Puritans, because they wanted to purify the Church of England of all remnants of Catholicism. The Puritans believed that many of the church's practices came from the pope in Rome and were not found in the Bible. These practices included kneeling to take Communion, making the sign of the cross, bowing when the name of Jesus was spoken, adorning churches with crucifixes and elaborate paintings of the saints, observing holidays in honor of the saints, and the saying of Mass, not to mention all the fancy vestments that bishops wore.

As William read more about Puritan beliefs and studied the Bible, he began to wonder if they might be right. He could find nowhere in the Bible where it said that the church should be controlled by a king or a queen whom Christians should follow without question. William had to admit that these were scary thoughts. A twelve-year-old boy was supposed to obey his elders and not entertain ideas about being disloyal to the queen's church. Still, the more he thought about it, the more curious he became about the Puritans.

One day a boy from the village confided in William

that he had been secretly going to Babworth, where a Puritan minister, the Reverend Richard Clyfton, was rector at All Saints' Church. Before he had time to think, William blurted out that he would like to go along next time. And so it was arranged. The following Sunday the two boys walked together ten miles south to Babworth, passing through the village of Scrooby, located on the Great North Road that stretched from London to Edinburgh, Scotland.

All Saints' Church in Babworth was a stone structure situated on a rise surrounded by graves, with trees beyond. The church had a square tower steeple that housed three bells at one end and a large, arched stained-glass window at the other. Tall, narrow windows ran along the side of the church. The church bells were ringing as William and his friend made their way inside through the porch and settled into a back pew. William was not disappointed with the service. He found Reverend Clyfton's style refreshing. The preacher had a bushy, white beard and preached with passion, quoted from the Bible, and prayed prayers that were not part of the Church of England's officially authorized Book of Common Prayer. After the service William talked with his friend all the way back to Austerfield about the church experience.

When he got back to the farm, his uncles were waiting for him at the door. "Where have you been?" Uncle Thomas asked.

William felt his cheeks turn red, but he did not want to lie. "To a Christian meeting," he said.

Uncle Thomas snorted. "The Puritans? Is that

what you mean? Stay away from them, do you hear? That misguided group will only land you in trouble."

William stood silently as his two uncles took turns trying to convince him to never attend another Puritan meeting. He was thinking of the verse Reverend Clyfton had read from the Bible during the service at All Saints' Church: "Blessed are they which suffer persecution for righteousness' sake; for theirs is the kingdom of heaven" (Matthew 5:10).

Still, early each Sunday morning William and his friend would set out on the long walk to church and back. William's uncles would glare at him and warn him not to go, but William felt drawn to the church in Babworth. Before long, his friend gave up on going, but not William. He walked alone the mile and a half to Scrooby, where he met up with the Brewster family. William Brewster, his wife, Mary, and their two children, Jonathan, aged nine, and Patience, aged two, lived in Scrooby, where William Brewster was the village postmaster. Together William and the Brewsters walked the rest of the way to Babworth.

William Brewster was twenty-four years older than William. As they walked, he liked to expound on all sorts of topics, and William loved to listen to him talk. William Brewster had studied at Peterhouse at Cambridge University, leaving in 1584 to work for Sir William Davison, secretary to Queen Elizabeth. During his service with Sir William Davison, he had spent time on diplomatic missions in the Netherlands, where he'd had the opportunity to see first-hand many of the religious reforms taking place in

Europe. Given William Brewster's hands-on political and diplomatic experience and his knowledge of religious reforms, William listened to him carefully, storing away many of the facts and arguments William Brewster put forth.

Although he served as the government's postmaster at Scrooby, behind the scenes William Brewster was influential among members of the Church of England in the area. Over the years, Queen Elizabeth had removed from their churches many Anglican pastors she disagreed with or did not like. William Brewster encouraged those congregations to seek replacement pastors who were godly men and hopefully shared the Puritans' belief in reform within the Church of England. He also urged church members to regularly attend services and actively help the poor and needy in their communities.

William's uncles continued trying to dissuade him from attending a church with a Puritan preacher. However, every time William studied the Bible or read one of the books William Brewster loaned him, he discovered more reasons to agree with what Reverend Clyfton preached each Sunday. Although St. Helen's Church was located not far from the Bradford farmhouse in Austerfield, William felt welcome at All Saints' Church in Babworth in a way he didn't at St. Helen's. He felt part of a community, something he'd been missing since his mother's death.

On March 26, 1603, about a year after William had started attending All Saints' Church, a messenger came galloping on horseback up the Great North

Road from London bearing news that Queen Elizabeth had died in her sleep two days before. The messenger was on his way to Edinburgh to announce to King James VI of Scotland that he was now also the King of England. Since Queen Elizabeth had remained unmarried throughout her reign, she had not given birth to a Tudor heir to the English throne. And since King James was related to the Tudors through both his mother and his father, in the absence of a direct heir, he was chosen to be the new king, becoming both King James I of England and Ireland and King James VI of Scotland.

The question on many people's minds, including that of now thirteen-year-old William Bradford, was what the new king would do with regard to the church. How would the king treat the Puritans and their call for reform within the Church of England? William Brewster thought relations between the church and the monarch might improve, that King James might extend to Christians the liberty to worship God as their conscience dictated. But it wasn't to be.

When King James took up residence in London, a group of prominent Puritan preachers compiled a manifesto titled the "Millenary Petition." This document listed thirty changes its Puritan authors wanted instituted in the Church of England. They were the same basic reforms Puritans had been advocating for years. When the manifesto was presented to the king, he called for a conference to debate the issues raised in the document. The conference was to be held at Hampton Court Palace in January 1604.

William Bradford and William Brewster, along with many other reform-minded Church of England members, waited anxiously for news of the outcome of the conference. When it came, it was not what they had hoped for. King James agreed to only one of the thirty points laid out in the petition. The king agreed to commission a new translation of the Bible into English. He stood firmly against all the other points presented and debated at the conference. What King James wanted was not a reformed church but a united church under his leadership. He wanted members of the Church of England to all be hearing the same sermons preached, reciting prayers from the same prayer book, and reading from the same version of the Bible. He wanted a Church of England that was not splintered by nonconformist groups or pastors who preached their own ideas and beliefs. To ensure he got the church he wanted, King James issued a proclamation against nonconformity, stating that all Anglican pastors must strictly follow the Book of Common Prayer. Those pastors who refused to follow this order would be removed from their position in the church.

Thus began a clampdown on the clergy and non-conformist congregations across England. And the man King James turned to for help in molding the church into the entity he wished it to be was Richard Bancroft, the new archbishop of Canterbury. Bancroft zealously enforced King James's new edict that pastors follow exactly the Book of Common Prayer. Those who did not were swiftly removed from their churches, and many were thrown in jail.

William watched as the work of building up the church in their area, which William Brewster had striven so hard to accomplish, was overturned. Pastors were being driven out because of their reformist ideals. The Reverend Richard Clyfton resigned from the church before he could be ousted. Now the members of the congregation had a decision to make: Should they stay at All Saints' Church at Babworth and await the appointment of a new pastor who would parrot the king's views, or could they take another path? That path soon emerged from the instructions in Paul's second letter to the Corinthians. "Wherefore come out from among them, and separate yourselves, saith the Lord" (6:17). They would become Separatists. Unlike the Puritans who continued to attend the Church of England in accordance with the law, hoping that one day the church reforms they sought would take place, the Separatists would have no more to do with the Church of England. At fifteen years of age, William Bradford knew this was both a radical and dangerous decision. He was convinced, however, that it was the only decision that those who held the same reformist ideals as he did could make.

Back at the Bradford farmhouse in Austerfield, William continued studying the Bible and reading books William Brewster loaned him. Although his family and others in the village mocked him for his extreme religious views, William began attending the Separatist meetings being held at Scrooby Manor under the guidance of William Brewster and Richard Clyfton. For the most part, the group was left in peace, but William realized the religious beliefs he had embraced put him and the others at odds with the most powerful man in England—King James. He knew that the Separatist group in Scrooby would not be left in peace for very long.

Chapter 3

Escape

In the fall of 1607, William Bradford found himself sitting in a jail cell in Boston in Lincolnshire. He was seventeen years old, and everything his uncles had warned him about was coming true. In fact, William was not the only one in jail. About one hundred members from the Scrooby Separatist group, including women and children, were there with him. Their crime: trying to escape England. The group had chartered a ship to take them from a remote area near Boston to Holland. Everything had gone well up until the time they boarded the ship. The ship's captain, an Englishman, had betrayed them to the authorities. The Separatists were arrested, stripped of their belongings, and thrown into jail. William wondered what would become of them all.

It was a gloomy time for William. His sister Alice and half sister Agnes had both died during the year, and William felt closer to the Brewster family than he did to any of his remaining blood relatives. Mary Brewster had recently given birth to another daughter, whom they named Fear because of the difficult times in which they lived.

After a long and uncomfortable month in jail, most of the Separatists were released and told to go home. The seven leading men of the group, including William Brewster and Richard Clyfton, were held over for trial. William Bradford returned to Austerfield uncertain of what the future held.

The winter of 1607–8 was particularly harsh. Word came from London that the Thames River had frozen over so solidly that a huge "Frost Fair" had been set up on the ice. And in Yorkshire, the ground lay under several feet of snow for weeks. The Separatists, including William, slogged through snowdrifts to hold secret meetings and wondered if it was possible to leave England without being captured.

By early spring 1608 it was settled: the Scrooby Separatists would try to escape again. On Tuesday, May 10, William packed a few clothes and some personal items into a leather bag, along with some books, the most important of which was his copy of the Geneva Bible. Once his bag was packed, he slung it over his shoulder and joined three other men as they set off walking. The men were headed for Grimsby Common on the south bank of the river Humber, near its mouth with the North Sea, forty miles to the east. They walked in silence, and as they made their way, other Separatist men joined them. Meanwhile, the women and children of the group, along with most of the luggage, had been loaded onto the *Francis*, a barge usually used for hauling coal. The group would travel down the river Trent to the Humber and meet the men at Grimsby Common. It had been secretly arranged that at Grimsby Common they would all board a Dutch ship and be taken to Amsterdam.

As he walked, William knew he was leaving behind everything to live in a foreign country. He would need to learn a new language, obey new laws, and find a new livelihood. William Brewster had told him that the Dutch did not farm sheep or plant the same crops as the English did. These were daunting matters for an eighteen-year-old orphan to contemplate. But more than anything, William wanted the freedom to practice his faith without interference from the king or anyone else. William Brewster assured him that things were very different in Holland. William hoped so.

The men reached Grimsby Common early on the morning of Thursday, May 12. It was cold, and a biting wind was blowing off the North Sea across the Humber. The men gathered by the river's edge, and that was when William and the rest of the men spotted the problem. The *Francis*, with about ninety women and children and their luggage already aboard, had arrived the night before. As the barge pitched and rolled in the rough water of the Humber River, many of the women became seasick and urged the barge captain to seek shelter in Stallingborough Haven, a swampy, sheltered inlet off the Humber. As the tide went out overnight, the barge became stuck on a mudflat. Now it would take till around noon for the incoming tide to float the barge free. The Dutch vessel the group had chartered was already waiting at anchor out in the main channel of the Humber to take the Separatists aboard and set sail as soon as possible. But with the *Francis* unable to be reached, the travelers could do nothing but wait for the tide to come in.

William watched as several Dutch sailors rowed a longboat from their vessel out in the Humber River toward him and the other men on shore. As they got closer, two sailors jumped out into the thick mud and pulled the boat in closer. "The captain's worried about waiting for the women and children," one of them yelled. "He wants to at least get the men aboard while we wait. Come on!"

Half the men, including William, waded through the mud and climbed into the boat. The sailors rowed them to the ship, where they climbed nets up the side of the ship and onto the deck. William peered over the side just as the captain yelled and pointed toward Grimsby Common. William's blood ran cold as he turned to see what the captain was pointing at. A group of armed militiamen was racing along the track toward the common, where the other half of the men waited.

"I'm not staying here to be arrested," the captain said in a panic-stricken voice, and then barked to his crew, "Bring up the longboat! Hoist the anchor and unfurl those sails. Let's be under way."

The wind was at the ship's back, and the vessel was soon sailing through the river mouth and out into the North Sea. William knew he would never forget the sight around him. Tears ran down the faces of the Separatist men as they looked back in horror, realizing that their wives and children and their fellow Separatist men were being left behind and they were helpless to do anything about it. Worse, those left behind were at the whim of an armed militia band. William felt their anguish.

The nightmare intensified as the ship sailed into the jaws of a huge storm in the North Sea. The wind blew them far off course, close to the coast of Norway. Huge waves battered the small ship, which pitched and rolled violently. When a wave rolled the ship onto its side and the crew began to yell that they were sinking, the Separatist men prayed hard. Slowly the ship righted itself. The men continued to pray.

When the storm began to abate, the ship was able to get back on course. Fourteen days after setting sail from the mouth of the Humber River, the ship docked in Amsterdam. Under normal circumstances the voyage would have taken four days at most. As he disembarked, William hoped he would never have to make another harrowing sea voyage like that again.

Immediately several of the men set out to return to England to see what had become of their wives and children. They were hopeful that if all was well, they could plan to rejoin the group in Amsterdam with their families.

Meanwhile, in Amsterdam, William and the remaining men were welcomed into a community

of Separatists who had fled there ahead of them
from other parts of England. The challenges William
faced in this new place almost overwhelmed him. He
had come from a village of two hundred people and
now found himself in a foreign city with a population of a quarter of a million. Everywhere he looked
he saw people and all kinds of activity taking place
in Amsterdam's narrow streets and along her many
interlocking canals. The first thing William needed
to do to support himself was find a job. The manu-
facturing of textiles was one of the main industries
in Amsterdam, and William soon found a job as an
apprentice silk weaver. The job didn't pay much and
it was tedious, but William was glad to have it.

Bit by bit, the members of the Scrooby Separatist group left behind in England began to trickle into
Amsterdam. They had initially been arrested and
their luggage confiscated, but the authorities in England didn't seem to know what to do with them and
had let them go. The authorities had also turned a
blind eye as various Separatist families left England
for Holland. Before long, all the group's elders were
safely ensconced in Amsterdam. Once the Brewster
family was settled, William moved in with them. The
other members of the group also found jobs in the
textile industry and set up households of their own.

Within a year, however, cracks appeared among
the Separatists in Amsterdam. One of their leaders,
John Smyth, began preaching that baptizing babies,
as Catholic, Anglican, and Separatist congregations
did, was wrong because there was no mention of
such a practice in the Bible. Smyth believed that

only adults who knew what they were doing should be baptized. Chaos followed among the Separatists as some members were rebaptized and others were not. It was all too much for the core group of Scrooby Separatists, who only wanted to live in peace and harmony. Reluctantly, they agreed that it was time to remove themselves from their friends in Amsterdam and start again.

In the spring of 1609, a group of about one hundred people, including William, the Brewsters, and another family, the Robinsons, moved to Leyden, twenty-two miles southwest of Amsterdam. Leyden was a bustling university city of forty thousand, built on thirty islands connected with 145 bridges in the Rhine River. From the moment he arrived, William appreciated the beauty of Leyden in comparison to Amsterdam. The city was also a center for textiles, and once again the men and women of the group found work in the textile industry. However, silk fabric was not manufactured in Leyden, and William found a job as an apprentice weaving fustian, a corduroy-like cloth made from linen and wool. William was now nineteen years old. He looked forward to the time when he would turn twenty-one, when he could sell the land and houses that were his inheritance in England and set himself up in his own business.

Life for the Separatists from Scrooby fell into a pattern of work, sleep, and worship. But though Leyden was a beautiful city, life there was not without its hardships. William lived with the Brewsters in a house located on Stincksteeg, or Stink Alley. The alley was dark and only five feet wide, and it continually stank. And it was challenging to feed and clothe everyone. Living in the city was more expensive than living in the countryside of Yorkshire. Because there were no fields in which to grow vegetables or raise animals, everything had to be purchased at the market. As a result, everyone had to work hard to raise the money needed to survive. Even the children, some as young as four years old, had to work. The truth was, if a family could not make enough money, they were in danger of starving to death, especially since the price of food at the market seemed to rise steadily. Thankfully, since Leyden was a university town, William Brewster was able to find steady work tutoring students.

In March 1611 William Bradford turned twenty-one and was able to inherit the land and houses his father had left him back in England. He didn't want to return to England to take possession and sell them. William Brewster helped him appoint an agent to sell the properties and send the money to him in Holland. When the money from the sale in England arrived, William was able to buy himself a loom and small house on the Achtergracht, or Back Canal, where he set up a weaving workshop. He also put some of his money toward purchasing a home for the Robinson family. Pastor John Robinson now served as the group's leader, and he was able to use the new house as a meeting place as well. The group of Separatists living in Leyden was growing steadily.

About the time of his twenty-second birthday, William became a citizen of Leyden and a guild member. By now he spoke and read Dutch and was resigned to the fact that he would probably never return to England to live.

The following year William took one more step in the process of settling down in Holland. He married sixteen-year-old Dorothy May, whose family was part of the Separatist congregation in Amsterdam. The couple married on December 10, 1613, in the magistrate's office in Amsterdam. Separatists did not marry in churches, since they could find no examples in the Bible where this was done.

William and Dorothy began married life together in William's small home beside the canal. Their life continued to revolve around their church and the loom, since William's weaving business began to flourish. In 1615 Dorothy gave birth to a son, whom they named John, after their pastor John Robinson.

By now seven years had passed since the Scrooby Separatists had immigrated to Holland, but things in their new home were not going as well as many of them had hoped. A number of the people lived in cramped quarters, where disease was a constant threat. Several children had died, including the Brewsters' new baby. Many families worked with linen, and over the years, tiny, wiry flax fibers had lodged in their lungs, making it hard to breathe.

Not surprisingly, the young people, most of whom had been too young to remember the England they left, rejected the hard labor their parents had raised them to do. This became a concern to William and the other parents. They could see that in many ways their children were already more Dutch than English, and they wondered whether their grandchildren would even see themselves as English, much less as English people fighting for their religious freedom.

The Scrooby Separatists had another matter on their minds. Over forty years before, the Dutch had revolted against the Spanish monarchy, who ruled their country. A long struggle for independence ensued. In the process the Dutch embraced Protestantism and an attitude of religious tolerance. The fight for independence dragged on for years until in 1609 a treaty went into effect between Holland and Spain, ending the fighting for a period of twelve years.

The treaty would expire in 1621, and as the Separatists in Leyden looked at their long-term future in Holland, they were concerned about what might happen when the treaty ended. They feared that war would once again ensue, and if the Spanish won, they would turn Holland back to being a Catholic nation. This was an intolerable thought. After all, they had fled England to get away from the tyranny of a state-imposed church. And normally tolerant Holland itself was beginning to be wracked by religious extremism as Dutch Calvinists and Arminians fought against each other, sometimes violently, for dominance in the country. Although their sympathies lay with the Calvinists, the Separatists did not want to be caught up in the conflict.

As the months rolled by, the Separatists at Leyden became convinced that they would have to move again. This time they would find a place where they

could live and practice their faith in an English settlement. The big question was, where should they
go?

Two possibilities came immediately to mind. One
was Jamestown, the British settlement established
in Virginia in the New World in 1608. But the settlers who went there had endured such hardships
that it became almost impossible to persuade new
ones to follow. In an attempt to save Jamestown, in
1616 King James I had announced that men condemned to death could instead go there to live out
their lives. Another option was Guiana on the northern coast of South America. Many of the Separatists
had read Sir Walter Raleigh's account of the place,
describing it as lush and beautiful, with many available resources.

These two options, however, were soon dismissed.
The harrowing stories of the struggles of settlers
to survive in Jamestown soured the group on that
notion. And when it was learned that many of Sir
Walter Raleigh's men had died in Guiana because
of the harsh climate and disease, and that the place
was controlled by Catholic Spain, the idea of going
to Guiana was also abandoned. However, by Christmas of 1617, William had made up his mind about
where he would go. He and Dorothy would join a
group of Separatists bound for the New World, not to
Jamestown but to somewhere else in Virginia where
they could build and shape their own community.

The first step toward making this a reality was to
commission two of their own, John Carver and Robert Cushman, to travel back to England to obtain

the legal documents and raise the money needed to reach the New World. It was now early 1618, and the men hoped to return with good news by the end of the summer.

Chapter 4

Decisions

As William shot the loaded shuttle through the warp threads on his loom, he thought about the many decisions that would need to be made before the group left for America. Which leaders would go? The congregation in Leyden was growing. It now had three hundred members who came from all over England. How many of them should go in the first wave, and how many should follow later? Would they be able to finance the trip? How many ships would they need, and where would they find them?

Looking down at his three-year-old son John playing on the floor with some empty yarn spools, William wondered what the child's future would be. Should they even take John with them or leave him with his maternal grandparents in Amsterdam? Was John too young to survive a long ocean voyage, even though others would take the chance with their children? And if they left John behind, how would Dorothy cope with the separation from their only child? William didn't know the answer to these questions, but he knew that he could pray and ask God to guide them all.

Letters from John Carver and Robert Cushman in England told a frustrating story. The two were in negotiations with the Virginia Company of London. The Virginia Company had been granted a Royal Charter, or long-term lease, for the Virginia territory in America. In return the company was charged with establishing and supporting settlements in the territory. To do this, the Virginia Company gave land grants to groups of settlers willing to pay their way to the New World to establish communities. John and Robert were trying to negotiate such a land grant, or patent, as it was called, from the company for the Separatists from Leyden. But the negotiations were proving to be slow and protracted.

That summer William learned that another group of Separatists in Amsterdam were on the move. Somehow they had already obtained a patent and permission to immigrate to Virginia, and 180 of them, under the leadership of Elder Francis Blackwell, were traveling to London to board a ship for America. Hearing the news made their own lack of progress in securing a land grant all the more frustrating for William.

In the end, the Leyden Separatist congregation decided to send William Brewster to London in an effort to hurry things along. Although he was the man who had the most experience with diplomacy, he also had one major strike against him. The year before, he had set up a printing press and started producing books that mocked the Church of England and its leaders, particularly King James. The Leyden congregation decided to send him to London anyway, hoping he met no one who had read the books he had published.

In May 1619 another blow struck the group's plans to move to America. William, who was now one of the elders of the congregation, received a letter from Robert Cushman. It started out in much the same way as most of his other letters, describing the difficulties he and John Carver faced in their dealings with the Virginia Company and its convoluted politics. It then went on to report something else. William's heart raced as he read.

> He [Captain Samuel Argall] brought heartbreaking news about the ship called the William and Thomas, which carried Elder Francis Blackwell and his people.
>
> They sailed too far south due to the northwest winter winds. The shipmaster and six crewmen were dying and it was a terribly long search for the Chesapeake Bay. The ship full of settlers didn't arrive in Virginia until March—six months after leaving England. Mr. Blackwell and Captain Maggner are both dead.
>
> Mr. Argall has informed us that, of the 180 people [who] were tightly packed on that

ship, 130 of them are now dead. They lacked fresh water and were afflicted with diarrhea.

When William read Robert's letter to the congregation on Sunday morning, everyone was sobered. They knew many of the people who had perished on the *William and Thomas* bound for Virginia. This could just as easily be their fate. William knew the sad news would cause many hearts to grow faint, but he encouraged the members of the congregation to stand firm. "Great and honorable actions are accompanied with great difficulties and may be overcome with answerable courages. . . . These difficulties are many, but not invincible," he told them.

Yet William and the others knew that getting to the New World safely was just the first of many equally dangerous hurdles they would have to overcome. Once there, they would have to contend with Indians, and they had heard a number of reports of how members of the Jamestown community had had to fight them. Also, the Dutch, Spanish, and French were contending with England for control of land in America. Given these realities, William quietly began making inquiries to find a military man who could go with them to America to help guard the group and teach them how to protect themselves.

Their first choice was Captain John Smith, one of the founders of the Jamestown settlement in Virginia. John had explored and mapped much of the northeast coast of North America. He had firsthand experience that would be invaluable to the Separatists when they reached the New World. However, the price he asked for his service was too high, and William kept looking. He found Captain Myles Standish, an Englishman who lived in Leyden with his wife, Rose.

Myles Standish had first come to Holland as a lieutenant in the English army when Queen Elizabeth chose to support the Dutch in their fight for independence from Spain. He fought in a number of battles and was promoted to the rank of captain. When the twelve-year truce between the Dutch and the Spanish was signed, he stayed on in Holland. William and several elders from the Separatist congregation met with Myles and discussed their concerns and needs for life in America. Captain Standish, a short, red-headed man, seemed competent and supportive of the group's goal and agreed to sail with them to the New World and serve as their military advisor.

Throughout the summer, more letters from John Carver and Robert Cushman in London told of the endless roadblocks put in their way as they tried to gather the backing and resources needed to make the perilous journey to resettle in America. While the Virginia Company was willing to grant a land patent to the Separatist group, the sticking point seemed to be the guarantee the Separatists sought—that they would enjoy religious freedom once they got there.

Everyone, including William, was relieved when a letter arrived from London announcing that the Virginia Company had agreed to grant them the land patent. It was for land in the northern reaches of the Virginia territory, near the mouth of the Hudson

River. Now it was time to find investors willing to pay for provisions and the voyage across the Atlantic Ocean. William and the others prayed that Robert and John would find the right people to help them. William Brewster was no longer able to help. The king had discovered that he had printed the banned books ridiculing him and the Church of England and called for William's arrest. As a result, William was now in hiding.

Negotiations with potential investors dragged on until everyone in Leyden was thoroughly discouraged. But when the Dutch government learned that the Separatists were planning to leave and go to America, they made them a tempting offer in January 1620. The New Netherlands Company promised the Separatists free passage to America, cattle, and the freedom to practice their religion if they would settle in the Dutch colony to be established at the mouth of the Hudson River. Although the Separatists would have preferred to remain under the English flag, they were so frustrated with the lack of progress in negotiations in London that they pursued the offer.

Just as they were about to sign the deal offered by the New Netherlands Company, an English merchant named Thomas Weston arrived in Leyden. He and a group of seventy investors who called themselves the Merchant Adventurers offered to support the Separatists' venture in the New World. The Merchant Adventurers would send the Separatists out and supply them with everything they needed to build a colony once they reached North America.

For their part, the Separatists would be required to repay the investors over time for all that was supplied to them and provide profits from farming and fishing. Once again John Carver and Robert Cushman entered into negotiations.

An agreement was reached, and a partnership was formed between the Merchant Adventurers and the Separatists from Leyden. In the agreement the Separatists were referred to as Planters, since they would be the ones who would go and plant the settlement. The terms of the contract between them required the Merchant Adventurers to provide ships and supplies to the Planters in exchange for seven years of work upon reaching the New World. During this time, any money the Planters made as fishermen and farmers would go toward paying the debt they owed to the Merchant Adventurers. When that debt was paid, all profits would then be held in escrow as shares of stock until the end of the seven-year period. At that time the profits would be divided between the Planters and the Merchant Adventurers. Although they were required to work to fulfill the agreement, the Separatists were allowed to work two days a week for their own benefit. At the end of the seven-year partnership, the Planters would own their own homes and land in America.

Now that they had a land patent in Virginia and a partnership agreement with a group of investors, it was time for the Separatists to start making some decisions. Pastor John Robinson decided to stay in Leyden with those who wanted to remain there. He promised to join the travelers in the New World as soon as possible. William and Dorothy agonized over whether or not to take their son John with them. They chose to leave him with his grandparents, in the hope that he could later sail to America with the Robinsons or another family from Leyden.

Mary Brewster decided to take her three youngest children, Fear, Love, and Wrestling (after wrestling with Satan), with her and leave the two oldest children, Jonathan and Patience, behind with the Leyden community. Her husband, William, was still in hiding in England, but in secret letters back to Holland he'd told his wife he would meet the family when they arrived in England.

The members of the Leyden congregation were left to pray and make decisions about who should go on the first shipload. Four men, Francis Cooke, Thomas Rogers, Samuel Fuller, and Richard Warren, left their wives behind in Leyden while they went on ahead. The wives would travel over once their husbands were settled in America. Another man, Isaac Allerton, decided to take his pregnant wife, Mary, and their three young children, Bartholomew, Remember, and Mary, along on the first ship. William Bradford and the others who were leaving began to sell their houses and possessions in Leyden in preparation for traveling, first to England and then on across the Atlantic Ocean to the New World.

In Leyden William and the other men met regularly to pray and talk and plan their next step in the process. At one of these meetings, they decided to pool much of the money they'd received from selling their homes and possessions and use it to buy a small ship of their own in Holland. This, the men reasoned, would save them money in the long term. They could use the vessel to cross over to England and then sail it on across the Atlantic. When they reached the New World, the ship could be converted into a fishing boat for the abundant supply of cod that swam the waters off the northeast coast of North America. In this way they would be provided with fish for the winter and hopefully have enough left over to salt and send back to England to sell to pay back their debt to the Merchant Adventurers.

William was put in charge of finding a suitable boat. He soon located a sixty-ton ship named the *Speedwell.* William was told that the vessel, although only fifty feet long, was well able to cross the Atlantic to North America. Far smaller and lighter ships than the *Speedwell* had crossed the ocean and made it back safely. The group bought the *Speedwell* and had it fitted with two new masts for the voyage. They also hired a captain and crew, who all agreed to stay on in America for one year.

After many delays, the day arrived for the seventy or so Separatists who had decided to cross the Atlantic and establish a new community in America to assemble at the small Dutch port of Delfhaven, where the *Speedwell* lay at anchor. The luggage was rowed out to the ship and loaded along with barrels of Dutch butter the travelers intended to take with them to the New World.

A large group of Separatists and friends from Leyden traveled to Delfhaven to say farewell. Some

Separatists even came from Amsterdam, fifty miles away, for the occasion. That night a large feast was held in Delfhaven, accompanied by prayer, singing, and many tearful goodbyes. As William looked around at the feast, he was overwhelmed at the sacrifices some of the travelers were about to make.

On the morning of July 21, 1620, the departing Separatists began being rowed out to the *Speedwell*. When it was their turn, William and Dorothy said a tearful goodbye to their five-year-old son John and climbed into the rowboat. William looked back at his son as they rowed away. He hoped that John would be able to join them in the New World before too long.

Pastor John Robinson came out to the ship by rowboat for a final farewell to the members of his congregation. He wished everyone well on the adventure that lay ahead. After embracing William, Pastor Robinson handed him a letter with instructions to read it to the group once they reached England. By then the tide had turned, and it was time to sail. Pastor Robinson said a fervent prayer for the group and commended them to God's care. He then climbed back into the rowboat to go ashore.

The *Speedwell*'s anchor was raised and its sails unfurled. The first leg of the journey to the New World had begun. They were headed for the port of Southampton in the south of England where they would join up with the other ship the Merchant Adventurers had chartered to make the journey across the Atlantic. In Southampton they would load the ships with the supplies and equipment the investors had promised to provide.

As the *Speedwell* set sail, William realized they had no time to lose. It was already July, and they were running very late. William had hoped that the group would have their crops planted and growing in the New World by now.

Chapter 5

Crossing Over

The *Speedwell* made good time to Southampton. William stood on deck as they sailed past the Isle of Wight and into the harbor. It was the first sighting of his homeland in twelve years. The *Speedwell* dropped anchor next to a ship named the *Mayflower*. This ship was one hundred feet long, beak-bowed, and about three times the size of the *Speedwell*. It was square-rigged with three masts and had high, castle-like structures fore and aft.

"Welcome to England!" William heard someone yell. He looked over and saw John Carver standing on the deck of the *Mayflower*.

"Is this our ship?" William yelled back.

"Yes, she's a fine vessel!"

William was sure that things were going well and they would soon be on their way to America.

Once the *Speedwell* was firmly anchored, William and Myles Standish were rowed to the *Mayflower*. After climbing the rope ladder and boarding the ship, William looked about. He saw many strangers on deck who seemed to be making themselves at home. A young boy rushed past him, chasing a dog.

"Greetings, Brother. Welcome aboard. How was your voyage?" John Carver asked as he reached out to embrace William.

"We had a prosperous wind," William replied. Then he frowned. "Who are these people? Are they Separatists like us?"

John shook his head. "Many things have changed since I last wrote to you. Decisions had to be made, and regrettably, Robert Cushman made them without consulting me or anyone else."

"What kinds of decisions?" William asked, trying to keep his voice calm.

John began relating what had happened. The Merchant Adventurers, led by Thomas Weston, had recruited fifty more people to join the Separatists in their new colony. They had not asked permission to do this. They didn't need to, since they were the ones holding the purse strings. Thomas had assured John and Robert that the people had been chosen carefully to add needed skills to the group. But according to John, this simply was not true. Among these "useful" people were four siblings, Ellen, Jasper, Mary, and Richard More. They were between the ages of four and eight and were the victims of a nasty divorce. Their father, a wealthy landowner, had told the court he did not believe that the children were his. Even so, he won custody of them and now, without his ex-wife's permission, had paid Thomas Weston to ship the four children out on the *Mayflower* to work as servants in the colony.

William was appalled. But there was more. Several young men had been hired as laborers, but they did not look as if they would take orders from anyone. And then there was Christopher Martin, one of the original seventy Merchant Adventurers, who was sailing with them to the New World to oversee their interests. He had his wife, Mary; a stepson, Solomon Prower; and his servant with him. The Merchant Adventurers had declared him to be the governor of the *Speedwell.*

As William shook his head, John quickly outlined the problems that he and Robert had had with Christopher, who was wealthy, opinionated, and used to getting his own way. The man had purchased supplies for the voyage without considering costs. As a result, the money had run out before all the necessary supplies and equipment could be purchased. When the two Separatists questioned some of his decisions, he refused to hand over his receipts, telling them that it was none of their business. William realized there was little they could do now. Christopher Martin and his domineering ways would have to be tolerated.

The only good thing William could see was that some of the new passengers had specific skills—skills that would be useful in starting a new colony. He realized that the Separatists had little to offer in that regard. Apart from Thomas Tinker, who was a carpenter, the other Separatists were involved in the cloth trade: dying, carding, spinning, and weaving. And before that, most had been farmers in England.

That night, as William sat down with John and Robert, he learned the details of the deal Robert had agreed to. Robert explained that Thomas Weston had brought some new investors into the Merchant Adventurers, and these investors wanted the terms of the venture altered. As a result, at the end of the seven-year contract period, only half of the settled land and property, and not all of it, as previously agreed upon, would revert to the Separatists. Also, the provision that each of them was to have two days per week to work on personal projects had been deleted from the contract. Robert said he'd had no choice but to sign the amended contract on behalf of the group. If he didn't, their dream of moving to the New World would have been over.

William was shocked by the new terms. They'd had a signed, agreed-upon contract, which they had negotiated with Thomas Weston and the Merchant Adventurers in good faith. Now it had been swept aside with the stroke of Robert Cushman's pen. "*You might have signed the contract, but I will not, and I doubt any other of our number will,*" William told Robert.

The type of people who had been added to their group was also a concern to William. How were these individuals ever going to work together with the Separatists to form a settlement on the other side of the Atlantic? Robert confirmed what John had told William earlier in the day: Thomas Weston had not asked their permission to add these people to the group, but they were powerless to stop him. Robert also told William that he thought it would be a miracle if they all got to their destination and started a plantation without everyone turning on each other.

William wondered if their whole venture had been doomed from the start. It was difficult to believe that God had arranged for these people to join them. William knew they now had no choice but to pray that everything would turn out all right. It was midsummer, and they needed to be on their way as soon as possible to avoid storms in the Atlantic Ocean and arrive before the cold of winter.

Things went wrong from the start. Thomas Weston arrived in Southampton from London, and he was unwilling to renegotiate some of the changed terms of the contract with the Separatists. In the end he stormed off, telling them that the Merchant Adventurers were not going to spend another penny on the voyage. This left the group with a shortfall of nearly one hundred pounds, and they were forced to sell off some of their food supplies, including the butter they had brought from Holland, to raise money so they could set sail.

William's spirits lifted when William Brewster was smuggled aboard the *Mayflower*. William Brewster would have to lie low until the ship cleared English waters, but William was greatly relieved to have his friend and one of the group's leaders back among them.

On Saturday, August 5, 1620, a month past their original scheduled date to leave England, the

Speedwell and the *Mayflower* unfurled their sails, headed out of Southampton Harbor, passing the Isle of Wight, and sailed into the English Channel. William and most of the Separatists were aboard the *Speedwell,* along with Christopher Martin, his family, and his servant. Most of the other "Strangers," as the Separatists had taken to calling those people the Merchant Adventurers had recruited, were on the *Mayflower.* In all, 130 passengers were aboard the two vessels. The ships sailed within sight of each other, but after a few hours the *Speedwell* sprung a water leak. Captain Reynolds kept William Brewster and William Bradford informed, and soon it became clear that the situation was dangerous. There was no way the *Speedwell* could safely undertake a long voyage across the Atlantic. The vessel headed back to land, and the *Mayflower* followed. The ships made for Dartmouth Harbor, where the *Speedwell* was examined. A shipwright recaulked the planking, but he could not find any reason for such a serious leak.

On August 23 the two ships sailed once more. This time they were three hundred miles out to sea when the *Speedwell* started to leak again. Captain Reynolds told the Separatists that he had no choice but to turn the ship around and head for the nearest port. Again the *Mayflower* trailed behind. It was a tense sail back—a race against time and tide, but the ship made it to Plymouth Harbor waterlogged and listing badly.

At Plymouth, Captain Christopher Jones of the *Mayflower* ordered everyone to stay aboard out of fear that the passengers would flee if given the chance. Those on the *Speedwell* quickly disembarked their vessel. Some who got off refused to set foot on another ship. Two false starts were enough for them. They opted to stay in England rather than risk a third attempt to cross the Atlantic Ocean. Among these were several families from the Leyden Separatist group, including Robert Cushman.

Once the skittish passengers of the *Speedwell* left the group, 102 passengers were still either committed to the joint venture or, like the More children and the twenty-five indentured servants, had no choice but to follow along. The group was made up of fifty-two men, twenty women, fourteen young children, and sixteen adolescents between the ages of twelve and sixteen. In addition the *Mayflower* had a crew of thirty. Besides William, only two other members from the original Scrooby group were aboard— William and Mary Brewster.

It was obvious that the *Speedwell* did not do well in open water, and the elders agreed that the vessel should be left behind and sold. It was of no use to them. But with it went their hopes of fishing along the East Coast of America and sending back fish to make a profit for their investors. Perhaps more discouraging was the fact that without their own ship, the group would have no way to escape or return to England or to a safer haven, if necessary. Once they reached America and the *Mayflower* sailed home, they would be alone with the Indians—and the weather. That was another big concern. It would be early winter when they arrived, and they had already sold and used up much of their food rations in the two false starts to the voyage.

As the men discussed their predicament, they realized that they would have to leave regardless of what lay ahead. The *Mayflower* voyage had been paid for, and there was nowhere in England for so many people to stay until spring.

William shook his head as he thought about the voyage ahead. The *Mayflower* was never intended to carry 102 passengers. In fact, it was not a passenger ship at all. It had been a "sweet ship," meaning it had been used to haul barrels of claret wine in its hold between Europe and England. Often wine would spill from the barrels during loading and unloading, splashing and soaking into the wood and leaving the *Mayflower* with a sweet odor below deck. Most of the group's luggage was stored in the vessel's hold.

Above the hold and below the upper deck was the gun deck, or the tween deck. This was where the passengers lived in a space fifty-eight feet long, twenty-four feet wide, and five feet high. There were cannons on either side of the deck and various hatches that provided access to the cargo hold below. There were also a windlass and capstan for hauling heavy items between the decks, and the main mast ran through the middle of the deck. All of these took up valuable space in the cramped living area. A thirty-five-foot-long, single-masted shallop that had been cut in four was stored there too. During the day, gloomy light seeped into the tween deck, but at night it was completely dark. In the open area left on this deck, the passengers found space to live, some sleeping in hammocks they strung up, others on the hard deck. Some used planks of wood to divide their space in an attempt to have some privacy.

William found a small space for him and Dorothy to live in and arranged their hammocks and bedding. Even while they were still at anchor in Plymouth Harbor, he could hear the timbers of the ship groan and the water slosh in the bilges at the bottom of the vessel.

On Wednesday, September 6, 1620, a month and a day after setting out for Southampton, William stood on the deck of the *Mayflower* as the anchor was hauled up. "It's not going to be easy, but God will go with us," he said, putting his arm around Dorothy.

William soon discovered how true that statement would be. Two days into the voyage, he experienced the closest thing to what he imagined hell to be. There was a cook aboard, but he served only the thirty crew members. The passengers were left to fend for themselves. Since they had nowhere to cook, they ate cold food: hardtack biscuits, dried beef, and cheese. Most of the passengers lost their interest in food early on. Many became seasick, and the space between decks soon stank of vomit. Others got diarrhea from living in such unhygienic conditions. The only place to go to the toilet was over the edge of the poop deck at the upper rear of the ship. But this was too dangerous at night and too far away for a sick person to walk. Soon the floor of the tween deck was slippery with human waste that slopped from the few buckets they used as toilets.

Under such circumstances, those below deck got to know each other fast. They had little privacy, despite the rough wooden partitions some had erected. Dorothy spent her time tending to three pregnant women aboard. When the passengers went up on deck during the day to relieve themselves over the side of the poop deck or just to see the sun, they were ridiculed by the crew. The crew were used to transporting cargo, not people, and especially not women and children. A sailing ship was a man's domain, and many of the sailors believed that having women aboard was bad luck. Not only that, but also they were taking the women and children to Northern Virginia, another place where they obviously did not belong. The whaling, fishing, hunting, trapping, and exploring that went on in this region were manly tasks.

One sailor in particular led the taunting of the passengers. He liked to tell those who were sick that he would gladly wrap them in cloth and bury them at sea and then "make merry with what they had." When the Separatists rebuked him for his callous taunting, the sailor would curse and swear at them. Then one morning the sailor himself became sick, and before the day was over he had died and his body had been thrown over the side into the ocean. William observed that many of the other sailors took note of their comrade's death, perhaps seeing it as the hand of God at work. And while the taunting didn't end altogether, it became much more muted.

After four weeks at sea, one of the Strangers, Elizabeth Hopkins, gave birth to a son. She and her husband, Stephen, named him Oceanus, after the vast ocean that surrounded them. Stephen Hopkins was the only passenger aboard who had been to the New World before. He had spent time in Jamestown.

Not long after the birth of Oceanus and about halfway across the Atlantic Ocean, the *Mayflower* encountered a fierce storm. The wind whipped the ocean into a frenzy of waves that beat the ship backward and forward and from side to side. For fear that his ship might lose its masts and the sails be ripped to shreds, Captain Jones ordered the sails furled. The bow of the *Mayflower* was headed into the wind, and the vessel was left to ride out the storm. As waves crashed over the ship, the decks warped under the strain, momentarily opening up gaps in the deck planking. Through the gaps, frigid seawater rained down onto the passengers crammed together on the tween deck, adding to the misery they were already enduring.

As the *Mayflower* rode out the storm, John Howland, one of the indentured servants aboard, crept up on deck for a few moments of fresh air. He had no sooner reached the upper deck than the ship rolled violently to one side, pitching him overboard. Thankfully, the topsail halyard was trailing in the water, and John was able to grab it and hold on firmly as the crew reeled in the halyard and dragged him back aboard. John was ghost white from fear and shock. Even the captain said it was a miracle he'd been plucked from the sea in such a storm.

As the *Mayflower* rocked under the strain of the storm, one of the main beams amidships supporting the upper deck began to bow and finally cracked. The crew were unsure what to do about the situation.

Some even suggested turning the ship around and heading back to England. William was not ready to accept that proposal. They had come too far to turn back.

One of the men from Leyden suggested they use the wooden screw jack the Separatists were carrying with them in the hold to force the cracked beam back into place. William watched as the men fetched the jack from the hold and set it beneath the beam. They slowly turned the screw until the beam eased back into position. The ship's carpenter hammered a post between the beam and the tween deck to hold the beam in place for the remainder of the journey. William breathed a sigh of relief.

Slowly the huge storm abated and the weather settled, though it was much colder than it had been before. Winter was clearly approaching. The *Mayflower* had been at sea for five weeks, but the battering the vessel had endured made it impossible to say when and where the ship would make landfall.

The voyage dragged on, taking much longer than it should have. The situation on the tween deck was becoming serious. Sickness, scurvy, pneumonia, dysentery, and various infections were spreading among the passengers. And then the first passenger, William Butten, a servant of Samuel Fuller, died. His death was not a surprise. William had been lying ill below deck almost since the ship departed Plymouth. His body was buried at sea, and the *Mayflower* sailed on toward land.

All the Separatists could do was wait, encourage each other, and pray for their safe arrival in the New World.

Then three days after William Butten's death, at daybreak on Thursday, November 9, 1620, the lookout called "Land ho!" William Bradford quietly thanked God for delivering them to America. They had been at sea for sixty-five long days. Everyone, including William, hoped that the worst was behind them, even though William knew that could not possibly be so.

Chapter 6

Footsteps in the New World

William Bradford had the same question as all the other passengers and crew: Where were they? This was not a simple question to answer. As he peered to starboard, William could see a ridge of hills and a forest that came down to the water's edge. How far off the Hudson River were they? Although several crew members and passenger Stephen Hopkins had been to the New World before, none of them recognized what they saw. Captain Jones recalled a map he'd seen made by John Smith six years before, and he and his two pilots talked together. They came to the conclusion that the *Mayflower* was off the coast of Cape Cod in New England, 220 miles north of where they needed to be.

"This is the most difficult part ahead," Captain Jones told William, shaking his head. "You might think we have risked life and limb getting here, but the most treacherous part is sailing a ship close to shore. There are no reliable maps of the coast between here and the Hudson River. We'll have to proceed cautiously. There may well be reefs and rocks ahead. I've heard tell that there has been more than one shipwreck in these parts."

"What precautions shall you take?" William asked.

"We'll use a leadsman," the captain said, and then went on to explain that the leadsman would be stationed at the stern of the ship and would let down a lead weight on a long rope over the stern to measure the depth of the water. Fully laden as it was, twelve feet of the *Mayflower's* hull sat below water level. If the water got to twelve feet deep, the vessel would run aground on a reef or a shoal. "We'll try not to sail at night, though that will be difficult, as the daylight hours are getting shorter. At least the wind is from the north." With that, the captain ordered the helmsman to bring the ship onto a southerly heading.

The *Mayflower* ran south, parallel to the cape and about three miles offshore. William stood on deck eagerly taking in the first look at their new home. Whales swam around the ship, and schools of tiny fish swam beneath it. Some of the young boys scrambled up the ropes and yelled down commentaries about what they saw.

For five hours the ship sailed along easily before the wind. The leadsman at the stern took constant depth measurements, calling them out to the captain. But at around one in the afternoon, the tide turned and the wind eased. The water began to churn and swirl around them. Eddies formed as the tide sucked huge amounts of seawater in toward the rocky coastline. Captain Jones feverishly barked orders to his helmsman and crew, trying to turn his ship and get farther out to sea and away from the treacherous reefs and shoals. The wind pinned the *Mayflower* against the turbulent current. After two hours of frantic activity by the crew to keep their ship from running aground, the wind began to turn to the south, allowing the *Mayflower* to come about and sail away from the dangerous current, reefs, and shoals. William said a prayer of thanks.

Once safely out to sea again, Captain Jones announced that they were turning back and heading for Cape Cod. "It's too late in the season and much too dangerous to make it to the Hudson River. Regardless of your land patent in Virginia, you'll be going ashore in New England," the captain said.

William's heart sank when he heard this. He could see trouble ahead. The indentured servants, at least the older men, were already talking about not being legally bound to their masters once they landed because they would no longer be on land belonging to England. Some of the Strangers, John Billington in particular, complained about all of the praying and keeping of the Sabbath that had gone on aboard ship. They hinted that if they were not on English soil, the Strangers would leave and form their own colony.

Had the Separatists sailed all this way, losing only one of their number, only to be torn apart by the bickering and selfishness of the Strangers? William tried to understand how the Strangers felt. Those who were not servants had come with the hope of earning their own land, something the Separatists wanted too. Somehow they all had to stay together long enough to get a letter back to the Merchant Adventurers in England explaining what had happened and asking them to secure a patent for their new land as soon as it was legally available. In the meantime, some kind of agreement that would satisfy both the Separatists and the Strangers had to be reached. If they didn't find a way to work together, they might not survive the fast-approaching winter, their first in the New World.

That evening, as the *Mayflower* drifted gently in the water off the elbow of Cape Cod, William Bradford, William Brewster, John Carver, several other men from Leyden, and several of the Strangers met to discuss the matter. William read them John Robinson's letter, which John Carver had read aloud to the group before they left Southampton. After listening to the letter again and discussing it, they all agreed that they should elect a governor to lead them, following the steps laid out in Pastor Robinson's letter. All men over the age of twenty-one would vote, regardless of whether they were a Separatist or a Stranger, wealthy or an indentured servant. Each man would promise to obey all the laws and decisions made by the elected governor. By the next day they had come up with a written agreement, or compact, which read:

In ye name of God, Amen. We whose names are underwritten, the loyall subjects of our dread soveraigne Lord King James. . . . Haveing undertaken, for ye glorie of God, and advancemente of ye christian faith and honour of our king & countrie, a voyage to plant ye first colonie in ye Northerne parts of Virginia, doe by these presents solemnly & mutualy in ye presence of God, and one of another, covenant, & combine our selves togeather into a civill body politick; for ye our better ordering, & preservation & furtherance of ye ends aforesaid; and by vertue hearof, to enacte, constitute, and frame shuch just & equall lawes, ordinances, Acts, constitutions, & offices, from time to time, as shall be thought most meete & convenient for ye generall good of ye colonie; unto which we promise all due submission and obedience. In witnes wherof we have hereunder subscribed our names at Cap Codd.

Meanwhile, the *Mayflower* was sailing north at a fair clip. By nightfall the vessel was off the tip of Cape Cod. Since it was too dangerous to sail close to the coast at night, Captain Jones ordered the ship to heave to and wait for sunrise before entering Cape Cod harbor.

The sun rose five minutes before the 7:00 a.m. bell on the *Mayflower* on the morning of November 11, 1620. Those men who were well enough assembled in the great cabin on the main deck, where the text of the compact was neatly written on a large sheet of parchment. John Carver was the first to sign the document. He had traveled on the ship with his wife and five servants. During the voyage, he had taken in Jasper More, one of the four More children being exiled from England by their father. John then handed the plumed pen to William. One by one, the men stepped forward, Separatists and Strangers alike, to add their names to the compact. Those who could not write their signatures marked an *X*. In all, forty-one men signed the Mayflower Compact. Several men were too ill to join them. John Alden, the *Mayflower*'s cooper (barrel maker), also signed the compact. He had asked the leaders if he could leave the ship and settle in the colony. The group was glad to have an industrious young man like John throw his lot in with them.

With the Mayflower Compact signed, the next decision concerned who to elect as governor of the colony. Christopher Martin had been governor of the *Mayflower*, put in place by the Merchant Adventurers. Until now it had been understood that his authority would extend to the new colony. But now, with the compact signed, the men had given themselves the power to guide their own destinies. No one wanted Christopher Martin to remain governor over them one more day. The Strangers and the Separatists agreed that the one man among them best fit for the position was John Carver. Now they had an agreement and a governor. It was time to see their new home.

When William emerged on deck again, the *May-flower* had rounded the tip of Cape Cod and now lay peacefully at anchor in the harbor. William looked around and saw a beautiful scene, one he hoped he would always remember. It was a clear day, the sea a steel-grey color, with some clouds overhead and a late fall nip in the air. On shore William could see sand and trees and flocks of ducks and geese.

Now that they were at anchor, the settlers were eager to step onto land, but they were also terrified of the Indians or beasts that might be lurking in the forest surrounding the shore.

It was time to bring out the thirty-five-foot shallop from the tween deck. The shallop had been cut into four pieces to make it easier to stow. The colonists hoped to quickly reassemble the vessel and use it to transport them to land. But after the ship's carpenter examined the boat, he informed the men that it had taken a beating crossing the Atlantic. It would take days, if not weeks, to repair the vessel and reassemble the four pieces.

The group then turned to the *Mayflower*'s longboat, which could hold sixteen men. Each man going ashore wore a corselet (a form of light body armor that included a metal breastplate), placed a metal helmet on his head, strapped a cutlass to his waist, and carried a musket. Most of the men carried matchlock muskets with long wicks that were lit by a match to ignite the musket's gunpowder. Myles Standish carried a more modern flintlock musket that used the spark from a small hammer hitting flint to ignite the gunpowder. William had to admit, the corselet and helmet were not particularly comfortable but were necessary for the men's protection.

The group set off in the longboat around noon.
When they reached land, they waded ashore, carrying their muskets above their heads. When William
Brewster reached the shore, one of the first to do so,
he laid down his musket and fell to his knees. The
other men followed his lead. "Blessed be the God
in heaven who has brought us over this vast and
furious ocean," William prayed. "You have delivered
us from the perils and miseries at sea and set our
feet on firm and stable ground—our proper place to
dwell. For this we thank You and bless You." After
the prayer, William Bradford stood up, not an easy
thing to do wearing his corselet.

Since most of the men had never fired a musket, Myles Standish demonstrated how to tamp the
gunpowder in the weapon, load the lead ball, light
the wick, and fire. He then commanded several of
the men to stand guard at the front and rear of the
group as the other men, their armor and weapons
clanking, set off walking in single file over the sand
dunes. Soon they were over the first row of dunes
and found themselves in a hollow filled with trees.
Some of the trees, such as birch, walnut, and holly,
William recognized right away, while others were
unfamiliar to him.

A little farther on, the group found a grove of red
cedar trees. Five men stood guard while the rest,
using a saw they had brought along, took turns saw-
ing off large cedar branches to take back to the ship.

The whole excursion took less than three hours.
As the sun was beginning to fade, the men carried
the cedar logs back to the longboat, loaded them in,

and rowed back to the *Mayflower*. That night the colonists had a fire in the sandpit on deck. As cedar smoke swirled and sparks flew into the crisp night air, William wondered how long it would take for them all to settle in to this new land. He particularly wondered how long it would be before he and Dorothy could send for their little son, John.

The next day was Sunday. Even though the colonists had many important things they could be doing, the Separatists took the day to pray and read the Bible together. For the first time since they had left England, the Strangers did not object. Perhaps, William hoped, the Mayflower Compact would bind them into a united group.

On Monday, November 15, 1620, everyone who was well enough wanted to go ashore. Loads of dirty clothes and bedding were rowed in first, followed by the women and children. It did not take long to find a freshwater pond, where the women set about scrubbing the clothes while the children ran along the beach. William could hear their laughter as he and fifteen other men marched off on a second expedition, this one overnight. Once again Myles Standish was in charge, and once again the men were all wearing their armor corselets and iron helmets.

About a mile down the beach, William spotted a group of men and a dog. At first he thought they might be others from the ship. Then he realized they were Indians. The white men surged forward, slowed down by their armor, as the Indians disappeared into the woods near the beach. "Give chase," Myles urged as the men rushed on. Within minutes William was huffing. He, like the others, had been cramped on the *Mayflower* for so long that he could not run far before getting out of breath. The men walked on, catching a glimpse of the Indians' trail from time to time. They kept heading inland until they ended up on the Atlantic Ocean side of Cape Cod. They were cold and exhausted and set up a camp on the beach, posting guards for the night.

William slept surprisingly well. This was his first night in months sleeping on solid ground without the rocking of the *Mayflower* beneath him. Early the next morning the men were up again, ready to pick up the trail of the Indians, whom they hoped to talk to. Instead, they found several mounds of sand. One of the men began to dig and soon unearthed a bow and some arrows that were rotting. "This must be an Indian grave," Edward Winslow said, moving closer to it. "We should put everything back and cover it over. If the Indians are watching, we do not want them to think we are grave robbers." William and the others agreed. The bow and arrows were put back in the grave, which the men covered over again.

Not much farther along, the men came across several patches of cleared land. This was a heartening sign, since it probably meant that crops had been grown there. There was a piece of wood with saw marks on it and a ship's kettle. William quickly realized that other Europeans had walked this ground before them. *What,* he wondered, looking around, *had happened to them?*

A little farther on they came upon a fresh mound. William could still see the marks where it had been patted down. Even though they had hastily covered the grave and left it, the group was curious to examine this mound. After posting guards, the men, including William, took turns digging. It wasn't long before they came across several beautiful woven baskets filled with ears of multicolored corn. This was not a grave but a storage mound for seed corn.

William immediately saw the value of the corn. Although they had brought seeds to grow peas, wheat, and barley with them from England, he already had serious doubts as to whether such plants would survive here on the other side of the Atlantic Ocean. Now, in front of them were at least thirty ears of corn that had been grown and harvested in America. What should they do?

The men discussed the matter. It would be stealing to take the corn, but they really needed it. Perhaps God had put it in their path? In the end they decided to carry the corn back to the *Mayflower*. Later, when the shallop was repaired, they would bring back something from the ship to trade for the corn. For now, they decided to name the place Corn Hill.

The men spent another night camped in the open. This time, because it was raining, they used tree trunks and branches to shield them from the weather. William and the other men spent an uncomfortable night huddled together trying to keep dry. The next morning they set out to cross to the bay side of Cape Cod. On this portion of their expedition, William served as the rear guard. As he made his way through some trees, he heard a whoosh.

Out of the corner of his eye, he saw a sapling spring upright. At the same time, he felt a tug on his leg and then toppled backward. Suddenly he was hanging upside down by his leg at the end of a rope. His helmet and musket fell to the ground. "Help! Get me down," William called to the men ahead. Moments later he heard footsteps running toward him. And then a great burst of laughter. "So, you found the trap, and it works" Myles said.

"You might have warned me," William replied.

"We thought you would easily notice and avoid it. But it appears you didn't," Myles said with a chuckle, reaching for his cutlass and cutting the rope around Williams's leg, sending him tumbling to the ground with a thump.

After scrambling to his feet and putting his helmet back on, William looked at the rope that had snared his ankle, the sapling that had sprung up, and the acorns scattered about and asked what it was he'd stepped into.

"Mr. Hopkins here, who has spent time in Jamestown, pointed it out to us as we passed by—without any of us stepping into it, I might add," Myles said, still chuckling. "He says it's an Indian deer trap. And very ingenious it is. Look at the quality of this rope that hoisted you into the air. It's as fine a rope as anything I've seen in Europe."

William studied it closely. It was true. The rope was finely woven and strong. He wondered what else the Indians might be capable of making.

After the group reached the bay side of the cape, they headed back to the *Mayflower*, where everyone was eager to hear the stories of what they had found.

The story of William being strung up in a deer trap was also told, and William found himself laughing as loudly as everyone else at his misfortune. It felt good to have something to laugh about for once, even if it was at his expense.

The men undertook several more expeditionary trips but could not venture far along the coast in the longboat. Yet from the trips they did take, they decided the area was not suitable for a colony. The soil was too sandy, and there was no source of running water or even a good place to locate a fort, if necessary. They needed to wait until the shallop was repaired to sail farther afield to explore.

On November 27, the shallop was ready to use. It had taken much longer than anyone thought it would to repair and put it back together. By now the tween deck of the *Mayflower* looked like a hospital. The passengers were in worse condition than they had been sixteen days before when they landed. Scurvy, caused by poor nutrition, was affecting many of them, dysentery was still a problem, and many of the men who had gone on the shore expeditions had come down with colds that turned to pneumonia.

Although Captain Jones was an honorable man who had promised not to leave until the colonists were well situated, many members of his crew made it clear that they were anxious to be on their way back to England before the ship's supplies of beer and food ran out. William was well aware that time was running out for all of them—Separatists, Strangers, and the crew of the *Mayflower*. It was imperative that they find somewhere to settle themselves, and soon.

Chapter 7

Across the Bay

By dawn the next morning, Tuesday, November 28, 1620, snow covered the *Mayflower* and icicles hung from the rigging. It was not good weather in which to explore, but William knew they had no choice. They needed to find the best place to plant a colony.

William carefully picked his way across the icy deck and climbed down the rope ladder into the shallop. He was grateful that Captain Jones was leading the group. Although the captain was not required to help his passengers, he was as eager as anyone to find them a place to settle.

Twenty-four planters, all those well enough for the venture, and ten of the *Mayflower*'s sailors sat shoulder to shoulder in the shallop as they plowed through high seas under sail along the shoreline.

This time there was no bantering. Every ounce of energy went into guiding the shallop. After fighting the wind for several hours, the men finally found shelter in a small inlet on the far eastern edge of Cape Cod harbor. The men anchored in the inlet to ride out what had become a nasty storm. As night fell, a numbing cold descended upon them. William's clothes were soaked, and his teeth chattered. He had not, in his wildest dreams, ever imagined that America could be this cold.

The next morning, the winds had died down enough for them to sail south in search of a harbor. They found one and named it Cold Harbor, as many in the group were suffering from frostbite by now. Some of the men stayed in the shallop while others, including William, got out and marched along the creek that emptied into the harbor. Five miles later, frozen to the core, they decided it was too shallow to be a good place to bring the boat. The men set up camp for the night and roasted six ducks and three geese that one of the men had shot as the birds flew overhead. With everyone's stomach full, Myles set several men as sentinels. The rest of the men lay with their feet close to the fire, hoping their shoes would dry during the night.

Six inches of snow fell overnight, and the men were ready to leave Cold Harbor behind the next morning. They headed for Corn Hill, hoping to find more corn. The ground was frozen, and the men hacked at it with their cutlasses. They were rewarded with a cache of ten bushels of corn, along with a bag of beans. Captain Jones volunteered to take the corn and the sickest men back to the *Mayflower* and return the following day in the shallop to pick up the rest.

William and seventeen other men trudged on under the leadership of Myles Standish. They kept a keen lookout for Indians, but they saw none. They backtracked to near where they had earlier found the Indian grave. Not far from it they noticed a patch of ground where the snow had melted and where three long boards lay. As William peered at the planks, he saw that they were ornately carved and had once been brightly painted. What was under the planks? The men were curious. They lifted up the planks and dug down. About a foot below the surface, they found a mat wrapped around two bundles. They unwrapped the larger bundle first. It contained bones covered in a red powder. One of the men lifted the mat out and raked through the bones with his cutlass. William was sure that everyone saw it at the same time—the skull—a human skull that still had hair and flesh on it, and the hair was blond. This was the grave of a European. The men looked further and found a sailor's canvas bag containing a sewing needle and a knife. They opened the smaller bundle, which held the skeleton of a child. There was no hair, blond or black, on the skull.

Staring at the two skeletons, William stood quietly, wondering who these two people were. The man could easily have been a survivor of a French ship that one of the *Mayflower* crewmen said was wrecked in the waters off Cape Cod five years before. But what about the child? Were they related? And how did they end up in the same grave? The men had no answers to such questions, nor to the one William hardly wanted to think about: How did they die?

A little farther on from the graves, the men came upon a group of Indian homes in a clearing. It was clear that the inhabitants had left them in a hurry. Fires still smoldered inside the round, dome-shaped dwellings, and freshly caught and cooked fish and deer meat were laid out. A large cooking fire was set up in the center of their dwellings, and deer skins were laid on top of bed platforms around it. William paid particular attention to the structure of the houses. The frames were made of red cedar saplings lashed together to form a dome, which was covered with birch bark. The top of the dome had a square hole to let out smoke. William marveled at how well the structures seemed to keep the bitter cold weather at bay.

After helping themselves to some of the cooked food, the men headed to Cape Cod Bay to rendez-vous with Captain Jones and the shallop.

Once they were back aboard the *Mayflower*, the men gathered to discuss their options. They quickly decided that what they had seen of Cape Cod so far was not ideal. Who knew whether the freshwater ponds dried up in the summer? Robert Coppin, one of the ship's pilots who had been to the area before, thought he remembered a suitable harbor and land across the bay. He said it was named Thievish Harbor, because an Indian had stolen a harpoon from his ship while they were anchored there. The pilot was sure he could guide the men to the harbor.

Meanwhile, Susanna White, who was aboard the *Mayflower* with her husband, William, and their five-year-old son, gave birth to another son, whom they named Peregrine. William thought the name, which meant *wanderer* in Latin, was a particularly appropriate one.

Sadly, any celebration at the birth of Peregrine was soon overshadowed by the deaths of the White family's servant boy, Edward Thompson, and six-year-old Jasper More. That same day, everyone aboard the ship was nearly killed. Fourteen-year-old Francis Billington, a member of one of the Stranger families, fired a musket at the rear of the tween deck near the gun room where the gunpowder for the cannons was stored. An open barrel of gunpowder sat beside him at the time. Sparks from the musket started a fire on the tween deck. Thankfully, several of the men were able to douse it before it set off the gunpowder.

On December 6, ten men were well enough to make one more attempt to find the right place to plant a colony. The colonists decided that if they could not find anywhere more suitable, they would settle at Corn Hill on Cape Cod. William was a member of the group.

The men started out at the river mouth they had previously explored and made their way around the coast. According to Robert Coppin, Cape Cod Bay was U-shaped and about twenty-five miles across. The group hoped to stay close to the coast of the bay as they traveled. They planned to be gone for about a week. As he climbed into the shallop, William didn't think it was possible for the weather to get any colder than the last time they had ventured out, but it did. As soon as the sea spray hit his coat, it froze into a hard, shiny glaze.

The men sailed along the shoreline, heading south until the sun began to set. It was around 4:00 p.m. As they made for shore, they spotted a group of about a dozen Indians huddled around a large black lump in the sand. When the Indians saw the shallop, they ran into the trees. The shallop landed, and the men quickly made a shelter of logs and pine branches. As always, they set sentinels and settled in to rest for the night. William could hardly sleep. It was unnerving knowing that the Indians were so close, and his body was numb from the cold.

When a watery sun rose above the horizon the next morning, William was ready to get moving again. This time the men decided to proceed along the beach on foot, with just a few of them following in the boat. They soon reached the black lump they had seen the night before. It was a fifteen-foot-long whale that had washed up on the beach. The Indians were partway through cutting it up when they had been disturbed the night before.

The men from the *Mayflower* marched into the woods, hoping to see where the Indians had gone. They found another burial ground but not much else. The days were short, and by the time they had marched on down the beach three or four miles, it was time to set up camp again. Once more they built a barricade of logs and branches and placed sentinels at the opening to their camp.

Sometime in the middle of the dark night, William

heard howling. Most of the men were awake and heard it too. "Don't worry, it just be wolves," Robert said. "I've heard them before in the New World." Some of the other sailors weren't so sure and shot off two muskets just in case.

The following morning, the men were up early and had already loaded most of their gear into the shallop when they heard bloodcurdling screams, similar to those they'd heard in the night and thought were wolves. Suddenly one of the sentinels leaped over the barricade, followed by a wave of arrows. "Indians! Indians!" he yelled as he took cover.

Myles and several of the men sprang into action, muskets at the ready, and began to fire at the attacking Indians, who numbered about thirty. William took his place at the barricade as well. Five of the men had stowed their muskets in the shallop, and they dashed for the boat, avoiding the onslaught of arrows as they ran. The Indians tried to block them, but Myles rushed out with his cutlass drawn and fended them off.

Once the men had retrieved their muskets, they dived for cover behind the shallop and opened fire. At first the barrage of arrows kept coming as the Indians advanced from the trees toward them. But in the face of the musket fire, some Indians began to fall back. One Indian, who seemed to be the leader, stood by a pine tree and shot arrow after arrow at the men. He wouldn't be deterred despite the musket balls that careened around him. That is, until Myles took careful aim and fired. The lead ball from the weapon smashed into the tree trunk right beside the Indian's head, showering the man with shredded bark. The Indian turned and ran into the trees. The remaining Indians followed him. The attack was over.

William, like the other men, was shaken by the encounter. The group lost no time in getting into the shallop and casting off. They continued sailing along the coast in the direction that Robert said led to Thievish Harbor. Soon another terrible storm broke out. Snow began to fall, hampering their visibility, but they sailed on. As they sailed, a wave broke the rudder off the transom of the shallop. The boat spun around in the wind until two sailors were able to get oars into the water over the stern and steer the boat back on course.

The men sailed on. Darkness was not far off. The men were talking about what to do for the night when the mast snapped in three, sending the sail into the sea. William and several other men hacked through the rigging with their cutlasses and hauled the sail into the boat. It was too precious to allow it to be lost at sea. They were an ocean away from a replacement. Without a sail, the men took to rowing the shallop. As they rowed, Robert encouraged them, saying he recognized the rocky cliffs and sweeping hills.

Suddenly there was a roar, and sea spray filled the air. William caught a glimpse of enormous waves breaking on the beach. "Lord, be merciful," Robert yelled. "I am mistaken, for I have not been this way to Thievish Harbor before."

"If you are men, row for your lives, or we will all perish!" one of the sailors barked.

The men pulled the oars even harder. Their effort paid off. Slowly the shallop came around and moved away from the pounding surf on the beach. By now it was dark, and the men rowed on until they came to a sheltered sandy beach. Robert unwound the anchor and dropped it into shallow water. "This will do," he said. "We will spend the night on the shallop. After the attack this morning, we'll be safer at sea."

While William thought Robert was right that they would all be safer in the shallop on the water, it was also much colder. John Clark, the *Mayflower*'s other pilot, declared, "We'll be dead of cold by morning." There was a murmur of agreement, and several of the men climbed out of the boat into the water and waded ashore behind John. Once on land they lit a fire, and that was enough for William. "Better to face an arrow on land than this wretched cold at sea," he said as he too climbed out of the shallop and waded ashore. The rest of the men followed his lead. Soon William was beside the fire soaking up its warmth.

As dawn broke the next morning, the men realized that they had spent the night on an island. And since John Clark had been the first man ashore, they called it Clark's Island. Thankfully, the storm had passed and the day was sunny. The men were able to strip off their shoes and tunics and set them out to dry. They decided to spend the day resting. Some cleaned their muskets, others lay on the sand and soaked in the sunlight, while three of the crew members cut down a long, straight tree and fashioned a new mast for the shallop.

That night William lay down contented: his clothes were dry and the fire was well stoked. As he drifted off to sleep, he realized that the following day would be Sunday, December 10, 1620. It was not only the Sabbath but also an anniversary. On that day seven years before, he and Dorothy had been married in Amsterdam. How long ago that seemed now. William hoped that the worst was over and that by their next anniversary they would be in their own small house with a fireplace, dried meat hanging from the rafters. Perhaps their son John would have arrived by then, along with Pastor Robinson and the others from Leyden. William wondered if there might even be another Bradford baby on the way a year from now.

Since the next day was Sunday, the men rested again, listened to an impromptu sermon, and prayed that God would lead them to a good place.

From Clark's Island they could see that they were on the edge of a sheltered bay. As soon as the sun was up on Monday, December 11, the men climbed into the shallop and once more set out to explore. The bay was surrounded by mostly sandy beaches. Two spits of land stretched out into the bay from either side, providing a sheltered anchorage for boats. Using a lead line, they sounded for the depth. The water was mostly shallow, but as long as a vessel was anchored farther out in the bay, it was deep enough for a ship such as the *Mayflower* to anchor in.

The men went ashore. Small brooks ran down to the sea from the rising land beyond the edge of the bay. There was shelter from the harsh wind, and even though they saw several patches of land where Indians had planted corn in the past, they saw no sign of Indian activity in the area.

Although the bay seemed not to be Thievish Harbor, which Robert had been leading them to and which he reckoned was farther north, the colonists saw little point in searching any farther. This bay was the best place they'd seen since arriving in the New World. It was time to sail back across Cape Cod Bay to the *Mayflower* to tell the others about what they had found.

Chapter 8

Plymouth Town

The group headed back to the *Mayflower* on Tuesday, December 12, 1620. The wind and tide were in their favor, and the shallop made it before nightfall. As William climbed the rope ladder up the side of the ship, he noticed people moving away from the railing. Then he saw William Brewster's face—it was ashen. William's heart beat faster. What had happened in the five days he'd been away?

"It's Dorothy," William Brewster said after helping William onto the deck. "She is with the Lord now."

"What? How?" William stammered.

"She slipped on the icy deck and fell overboard. The crew used a hook to try to rescue her, but it was too late. She drowned. Dorothy saw the New World, but she was not destined to live in it."

William sat on the deck and held his head in his hands. His twenty-seven-year-old wife and mother of their son was gone. Dead! The news was hard for him to take in.

Later that night William learned that Dorothy was not the only person to have died while the men were away exploring. James Chilton, who was on board with his wife and youngest daughter, had taken ill and died. William tried hard to accept these deaths, but it was frightening. Since anchoring in Cape Cod harbor a month ago, four people had died. The group could not afford to lose one more person.

The next morning, the men from the exploring party presented their impressions of what they had seen and where they thought the group should land and settle. By now so many of the passengers and crew were ill that it took Captain Jones and the healthy crew members two days to prepare the *Mayflower* to sail across Cape Cod Bay to the harbor the men had discovered.

Sleet was falling on Friday morning, when Captain Jones gave the order to raise the anchor and unfurl the sails. A stiff breeze blew as the *Mayflower* left Cape Cod harbor behind. William stood at the stern, staring down at the water. His dream of a happy home across the bay with Dorothy and John was left in the vessel's wake.

When the *Mayflower* reached the other side of the bay, a strong wind from the northwest prevented the ship from entering the harbor. The ship anchored a mile and a half offshore. On Saturday the wind was favorable, and the *Mayflower* entered the harbor and anchored. Since the next day was the Sabbath, everyone stayed aboard.

On Monday, December 18, 1620, a group of men, including William, went ashore. They walked the beach, explored, and talked about the best place to build their settlement, which they were going to call Plymouth Town after the last port they left in England. They decided on a location beside a freshwater brook that ran down into the harbor. The brook would provide an adequate supply of water for their needs. Behind their chosen site was a small hill, which they were soon referring to as The Mount. On top of The Mount they would be able to post guards and hoped to install a cannon to help defend their community against any attacks from land and sea.

Now that they had chosen a location for Plymouth Town, the colonists were anxious to get to work. However, a strong northwesterly wind kept them cooped up aboard ship for several days. By now the situation on the tween deck of the *Mayflower* had become nightmarish. Almost everyone's clothes and bedding stank from repeated rounds of vomiting and diarrhea. And because of their poor nutrition, scurvy was rampant among the passengers. Richard Bitteridge, one of the single men aboard, died at this time, and his body was laid on deck to be taken ashore for burial. But before they could do that, a tiny body was lying beside Richard's—Isaac and Mary Allerton's baby, who did not survive birth. William hoped that when the men went ashore again, they could quickly build enough shelters to get everyone off the ship and onto land where the air was fresh, not fetid and disease-ridden like that on the tween deck.

On Saturday, December 23, the weather had cleared enough for twenty men to go ashore. They loaded shovels and axes into the shallop, along with the two dead bodies, and headed for Plymouth. Once Richard's and baby Allerton's bodies were buried in shallow graves, some of the men set about cutting down trees and clearing bushes. As they worked, William could see smoke rising in the distance from a large fire. It reminded him that they were not alone in this wilderness, which was also inhabited by Indians. William wondered when their paths might cross again.

That night they returned to the *Mayflower* with fresh water and juniper branches to burn. The following day was Sunday, and the group stayed aboard the ship to observe the Sabbath. The next day they went ashore to resume their work. Although it was December 25, Christmas Day, it was not a day the Separatists celebrated. To them it was just another Saint's Day promoted by the Catholic Church and the Church of England. Although there were some Anglicans aboard the *Mayflower*, they did not insist on recognizing Christmas Day either. There was too much work to do if they hoped to survive the winter.

The first building the men worked on was the common house, a structure about twenty feet square that they intended to use to store food, gunpowder, and other supplies. Progress was slow. Only one of the Separatists had carpentry skills. William was particularly grateful when John Alden, the ship's twenty-one-year-old cooper, joined them on the building project. By the first week of January, the common house was finished. Each family was then allotted a small plot of land thirty-two feet wide and fifty feet deep. The plots were situated on either side of the track the settlers had cleared from the waterfront up to the side of The Mount. The men then began building one-room cottages on the plots for the family households. In all, nineteen cottages would be needed to house everyone, since the single men and boys were assigned to live with various families.

The men used the same simple construction method that poor farmworkers in England used to build their dwellings. Each cottage, with a dirt floor and covering an area about twenty feet by twenty feet, consisted of a post-and-beam frame with a thatched roof. The walls were made of wattle and daub. The wattle consisted of mats of thin, woven saplings that were attached to the post-and-beam frame. The daub, a mixture of mud, sand, and straw, was applied over the frame and left to dry hard. Each cottage had a large fireplace about ten feet long and four feet deep and a small window made of parchment paper soaked in linseed oil. The window let some natural light in, but generally the cottages were gloomy inside.

As the men worked, the number of cottages needed began to decrease. As winter progressed, whole families began to die of scurvy, pneumonia, and dysentery. Christopher Martin, the governor of the *Mayflower* and the Merchant Adventurers' representative, died on January 8, 1621. In fact, the newly finished common house not only was used for storage but also doubled as a hospital for the sick, with usually six or seven ill people in it at a time. It wasn't long before William was one of them. Despite the sickness around him, William had remained relatively healthy since leaving England. However, as he worked away on one of the cottages, he was overcome with severe pain and collapsed. When he regained consciousness, he was lying in the common house with other sick members of the community. Unsure of what he was suffering from, he wondered if he might be the next colonist to die.

William's life hung in the balance, and then slowly he began to recover—but not before he was nearly killed in another way. Sparks from the fire in the fireplace set the thatched roof of the common house ablaze. As the roof burned, fiery twigs fell into the room and onto the sick patients, the barrels of gunpowder, and the charged muskets stored there. William was certain the whole place would explode, but the quick action of the men outside saved the day. The men managed to douse the fire quickly. William was relieved to be alive and also glad that the common house had not been completely destroyed. The thatched roof was burned, but not the walls. The roof was quickly replaced.

As his health slowly improved, William was glad to be able to leave the common house. Many others, however, were not able to leave. The situation became grimmer by the day. Myles Standish's wife, Rose, died, followed by the two small More girls,

Oceanus Hopkins, Mrs. Chilton, Christopher Martin's wife and stepson, and Isaac Allerton's wife, Mary. Burying the dead became a problem. Not only was the ground frozen, but also William and the other men were concerned about the Indians discovering just how few people remained in the settlement. They took to burying the bodies of fellow colonists in unmarked graves at night, sometimes two or three at a time.

William had been sure there would be tests for the Separatists, but he had no idea they would have to sacrifice so much so soon. Still, he clung to his faith in God.

More testing was to come. Torrential rain lashed the settlement, dissolving the daub the men had hoped would make the cottages waterproof. Everything was saturated, and still more people died. Given the harsh weather, Captain Jones had decided to keep the *Mayflower* at anchor in the harbor through winter, but now deaths among crew members were as common as those among the ship's passengers. The captain told William that he hoped enough sailors would be alive in the spring to sail the vessel back to England.

During this time, the thought of an Indian attack was never far from William's mind. But the truth was, the colonists rarely saw Indians. There was always the smoke from fires in the distance, but the Indians made no contact with the colonists. Captain Jones reported seeing two Indian men watching the *Mayflower* from Clark's Island. Two weeks later, one of the colonists was out hunting when twelve braves walked past him. They didn't seem to see him hiding in the reeds. Once they had passed, the man ran to sound the alarm. He told two other men cutting down trees in the woods of the encounter, and they fled back to Plymouth, leaving their tools behind. No attack on the settlement occurred, but when the two men returned to the woods to resume their work, their tools were gone. William wondered why the Indians were ignoring them. Were they waiting for the right time to mount a surprise attack on the settlement or to see if the colonists would all be dead by summer?

Although the Indians hadn't attacked, the colonists decided it was prudent to prepare themselves in case they did. They leveled an area at the top of The Mount, and Captain Jones gave them several of the *Mayflower*'s cannons. The cannons were brought ashore, and the healthy men dragged them up The Mount. It was hard work. Each cannon weighed about half a ton, and it took some maneuvering to get them set in place. But once set up, each cannon was able to fire a three-and-a-half-inch iron cannonball a distance of seventeen hundred yards.

On Saturday, February 17, 1621, the men of the colony met to discuss the details of how to defend their settlement in case of attack. Myles Standish was laying out his plan when William and several of the men noticed two Indians standing atop the low hill on the south side of the brook, about a quarter of a mile from their position. The settlers and the Indians stared at each other for a few moments, and then the two Indians motioned for them to come over to them. Myles and Stephen Hopkins offered to go and walked off in the direction of the low hill. After crossing the brook, Myles laid down his musket as a sign they came in peace. The two settlers were about to climb the hill when the Indians turned and left. It was clear from the noise they made as they left that many more Indians had been hiding behind the hill. The sound made William glad that the cannons were in place, just in case one day the Indians decided to attack rather than leave.

Two weeks later, in early March, William noted that the wind was blowing from the south and it felt warmer than usual. He heard a cacophony of birds chirping in the forest. The weather was beginning to change—spring was on its way. The harsh, cold winter would soon be over, and the settlers would be able to begin planting seeds and growing crops around Plymouth.

After having their first meeting to discuss military matters interrupted by the two Indians on the hilltop, the men decided to meet again on Friday, March 16. The day was sunny, and the group decided to gather outside to enjoy the weather. The meeting had barely begun when an Indian man walked into Plymouth and down the track between the cottages toward the men. He was tall and seemed unafraid as he walked. The man was also completely naked except for a leather strap with a short fringe tied around his waist. He was armed with a bow and two arrows. After walking right up to the gathered men, he stopped and spoke in English. "Welcome, Englishmen!" he said.

William was taken aback, as were the other men. Who was this Indian who spoke to them in English? His name was Samoset, and he explained that he was the subchief of a tribe that lived farther on up the New England coast. Though Samoset's English was broken, by listening carefully William was able to understand what he was saying. Samoset said that for years English fishermen had been visiting the region of the coast where he was from. Through interacting and trading with these fishermen, he had learned to speak their language.

It turned out that Samoset had also developed a liking for English food and drink. Soon after arriving at the settlement, he asked the colonists for one of their drinks. The colonists handed him a filled mug. They also served him biscuits, cheese, pudding, even a piece of mallard duck they had recently roasted. Samoset ate and drank with relish.

Samoset stayed through the afternoon, talking with the men and answering their questions as best he could. William listened closely as Samoset told them that local Indian tribes were joined together in a confederation that formed the Wampanoag nation. The Wampanoags were a strong group led by a man named Massasoit, who was chief of the Pokanoket tribe. They were located about forty miles to the southwest on Narragansett Bay. Samoset also explained that this place they called Plymouth was called Patuxet by the Indians and had been home to a tribe of the same name. However, all but one member of the Patuxet tribe had died from a plague that ravaged the area four years before. Now William understood why there was cleared land around them where Indians had once grown corn.

As darkness fell, Samoset was reluctant to leave, and he spent the night with Stephen Hopkins and his family in their cottage. The following morning he left the settlement carrying with him a knife, bracelet, and ring the colonists had given him as gifts. After he was gone, William tried to piece together all the information Samoset had given them about the Indian tribes of the region. This information was valuable. After all, these tribes were their closest neighbors.

Two days later Samoset returned, this time bringing with him five Wampanoag men. After eating with the colonists, the Indians proceeded to entertain their hosts with traditional songs and dances. As a gesture of goodwill, they also produced the tools that had gone missing in the woods back in early February. They then laid out some beaver pelts to trade. Since it was Sunday, the colonists told their guests they would not trade on the Sabbath. If the group came back in a day or two with more pelts, however, they would trade for them all. Already William was thinking about how much money such pelts would fetch in England. Perhaps this was a way to begin paying off what they owed to the Merchant Adventurers.

The five Wampanoag men departed, but Samoset stayed behind at the Plymouth settlement. Four days later, when his companions had not returned with more beaver pelts to trade, Samoset was dispatched to see why they had not returned. The next day, Thursday, March 22, Samoset returned to Plymouth, this time accompanied by an Indian man named Squanto. To the colonists' amazement, Squanto spoke far better English than Samoset. He said he was the sole survivor of the Patuxets, who once occupied the land on which the colonists had settled.

Squanto explained that in 1605 he had been kidnapped by a British explorer and taken to England, where he learned to speak and understand the English language and English ways. In 1614 Squanto returned back across the Atlantic, serving as translator for Captain John Smith on his expedition to map the coast of New England. At the end of the expedition, John Smith released him to his tribe.

Soon after Squanto returned home to Patuxet, he and twenty other Indian men were kidnapped by a British captain who took them to Spain where they were sold as slaves. Squanto was purchased by a group of Spanish monks, who set him free in 1616. He then found his way back to England and in late 1619 arrived in Newfoundland by ship from England. He immediately made his way south to Patuxet. He was excited to see his friends and family again, but when he reached his village, all that remained were barren fields. Every other Patuxet from his village was dead from disease.

As William listened to Squanto's tale he was amazed. This Indian had seen more of the world than he had. Squanto had endured voyages across the Atlantic and understood European ways. William felt an affinity with Squanto, who, like William, had experienced the death of close family members. The two men, even though surrounded by others, were in a strange way alone in the world. William also saw Squanto as a special instrument sent by God as a bridge between the colonists and the Indians. In this way, Squanto's sudden appearance was something beyond William's expectations.

The appearance of two more Indians atop the low hill on the south side of the brook was about to stretch William's expectations still further.

Chapter 9

Coexisting

"They are Ousamequin and his brother, Quade- quina. Ousamequin is also known as Massasoit, which means Great Chief," Squanto said, explaining who the two men at the top of the hill were.

"Why do you think they have come?" William asked.

"Massasoit is chief of the Pokanoket tribe and leader of the Wampanoag confederation. Perhaps they have come to make peace."

William had doubts about this suggestion when sixty braves—more Indians than the entire popula- tion of Plymouth—appeared on the hilltop with Mas- sasoit and his brother.

"The Wampanoag are made up of the remnants of many tribes. After the great sickness, few leaders were left. Each tribe owes Massasoit their loyalty but not their unquestioning obedience," Squanto went on.

The Indians came no closer than the top of the hill, and William and the other men of the community discussed what to do. Perhaps it was best to do nothing—or to fire the cannons to frighten them away. Squanto suggested that one of the men approach Massasoit and his men. The settlers quickly agreed that Edward Winslow should go up and invite Massasoit to come and meet with them in the settlement.

Edward put on his corselet of armor and his helmet and strapped a cutlass to his side. As he crossed the brook and climbed the hill, William sensed that everyone in Plymouth was holding their breath. Would the Indians attack Edward or welcome him? From what William could see at the top of the hill, the chief and his brother were listening to what Edward was saying. A few minutes later, Massasoit and several of his braves walked down the hillside to Plymouth while Edward stayed behind with Quadequina.

As Massasoit got closer, William studied the man who could obliterate their small community. The chief walked with long, confident strides, his head held high. He wore a fringed leather strap around his waist, and a deerskin was draped over one shoulder. As he got closer, William could see a chain of bone beads around his neck. He wondered if they were human or animal bones. The bodies of all of the Indians were decorated. Massasoit's face was a red color, and white markings adorned his body.

Meanwhile several of the Plymouth colonists had

spread a green rug on the dirt floor of an unfinished cottage and arranged several cushions for Massasoit and Governor Carver to sit on. Massasoit was shown into the cottage. Once Massasoit was seated, John Carver, wearing his purple governor's robe, emerged from his cottage. He was escorted by two Plymouth residents, one carrying a trumpet, the other a drum. The three men marched to the cottage where Massasoit sat. Following a trumpet salute and drum roll, the governor walked inside. John Carver reached out and kissed the back of Massasoit's hand. William hoped that the gesture would be taken as a peace sign. Massasoit then kissed the governor's hand. The men both sat on cushions, and John offered Massasoit a cup of brandy. With Squanto serving as translator, Governor Carver and Massasoit began to talk. Before long the two men had agreed upon a simple peace treaty and mutual-assistance pact.

William, who had been listening to the proceedings, was pleased with the terms. If the treaty was followed by both sides, he could see the Indians and the colonists living side by side. Under the terms of the agreement, the Wampanoags and the settlers would not hurt or attack one another. If an Indian broke the peace, he was to be sent to the Plymouth settlement for punishment. Likewise, if a colonist did the same, he was to be sent to the Wampanoags to be punished. The governor promised that the colonists would always enter Sowams, Massasoit's village, unarmed. In exchange, the Indians visiting Plymouth would leave their weapons outside the settlement. The two sides also agreed to come to each other's assistance if either of them was attacked by another tribe or outsiders.

Once the peace accord was settled and agreed upon, Massasoit and his entourage left Plymouth. Soon Edward Winslow, who had remained with the chief's brother, returned unharmed. William was optimistic about the accord with the Wampanoags. The colonists did not have to fear Indian attacks. This was especially important since spring was coming. It would soon be time to begin planting crops. Food was still in short supply, and more so, since they'd had to feed Samoset, Squanto, and several other braves. But hope was in the air that the worst was over.

The arrival of warmer weather brought a decrease in the number of people dying. The winter had extracted a cruel toll on both Separatists and Strangers alike. The *Mayflower* had departed England with 102 passengers aboard, and now only half of them were alive. Of the original fifty Separatists on the ship, only nineteen—eight men, three women, and eight children—were still alive. The members of four families from Leyden lay buried in unmarked graves outside the settlement. The Brewsters were the only Separatist family not to have suffered a death thus far.

On Thursday, April 5, 1621, William and the other colonists who'd survived the winter stood on the shore of Plymouth harbor and watched as the *Mayflower's* anchor was hauled up and its sails unfurled. The vessel came about and headed east. After being laid up for nearly five months in America, the ship was on its way back to England. Aboard was a skeleton crew, since the cook, the boatswain, the gunner, three quartermasters, and more than a dozen sailors had all died. John Alden, the ship's cooper, was not aboard, nor were two other *Mayflower* sailors who had been hired to stay on in the settlement for one year and help until more men arrived from Leyden.

William knew that the Merchant Adventurers back in England would be expecting the settlers to have loaded the *Mayflower* with pelts, timber, and other valuable items. However, all they were sending back were rocks from Plymouth beach that were being used as ballast. The colonists were too weak from trying to secure a foothold in a strange land to fell trees and saw them into clapboards, and they hadn't had enough time to set up a brisk trade for pelts. Not that they had much to trade for pelts in the first place.

The group had also sent with Captain Jones a map showing exactly where they had settled and requesting that the Merchant Adventurers secure an official patent for the land they now called home.

As the *Mayflower* faded from view, William knew that it marked the end of an era. The members of the tiny colony had always known that the ship was there as a lifeline to transport them back across the Atlantic to England if necessary. Now that lifeline had been severed. The nearest English community in North America was five hundred miles away in Jamestown, much too far to be of any practical help if the need arose. The fifty men, women, and children of Plymouth were alone, perched on the edge of a vast and unexplored continent. For now, they appeared to have secured the trust of a tribe of Indians, but how long would that trust last, and how strong was the bond?

About three weeks after the *Mayflower* set sail, Squanto declared that it was time to plant corn. Everyone in the community was expected to help as the settlers followed Squanto's directions. The process was complicated. Squanto explained that the soil in the area was poor and the corn seeds needed to be fertilized. He showed them, as the first step, how to construct fish traps to catch the herrings that teemed in the brook as they headed upstream to spawn. He taught William and the others, once they had caught the herrings, how to mound the soil. Into the center of each mound he placed several herrings and some corn seeds. As the fish rotted, they would provide fertilizer for the twenty acres of corn. Squanto also showed the people how to plant beans and squash seeds between the rows. These would grow and twine around the cornstalks, providing shade for the growing corn. The colonists also planted six acres of English barley and peas.

As the men worked mounding dirt with hoes, John Carver complained of a terrible headache. William and several others rushed to his side and helped him back to his cottage to lie down and rest. The governor of Plymouth Colony did not speak another word or leave his bed again. By the end of the week he was dead.

Governor Carver's funeral was the first to be openly held at Plymouth, with everyone in attendance. The men fired off a volley of shots in honor of their governor as they buried his body. Once the funeral was over, everyone's eyes seemed fixed on the future: Who would replace John Carver? William's name was put forward. William was surprised, since he was not the oldest or the most educated in the group. Still, he knew that someone had to step forward. He agreed to be nominated as long as Isaac Allerton could serve as his assistant. The men voted the following day, and William Bradford, the boy from Austerfield in South Yorkshire, became the second governor of Plymouth Colony. He was thirty-one years old.

One of William's first official duties, on May 12, 1621, was to perform a wedding. During the winter, Edward Winslow's wife, Elizabeth, had died, as had Susanna White's husband, William. The two survivors decided to marry. Since the Separatists believed marriage to be a legal affair and not a religious one, it became William's job to marry the two. The wedding was a celebration of hope for the future as Edward and Susanna joined together to parent Susanna's two sons, five-year-old Resolve and baby Peregrine.

Shortly after the wedding, John Carver's widow, Catherine, also died. William and many in the community thought she died from a broken heart following her husband's death.

William's days were now taken up with making decisions and presiding over disputes, of which there were many. One of William's first decisions related to John Howland, the man who had been pulled from the sea after falling overboard during the voyage from England on the *Mayflower*. John was the only surviving servant of John and Catherine Carver. Now that the Carvers were both dead, it fell on William to decide what should happen to their servant. In the end, William believed the fairest thing to do was to declare John Howland a free man and allow him to have part ownership of his former master's share in the company.

Other matters were more contentious. John Billington hated doing his share of the work and got into fights with Myles Standish about practicing military drills. And two of Stephen Hopkins's servants, Edward Doty and Edward Leister, got into an argument that ended in a duel. Both men were injured as a result, and William ordered them tied together until they worked out their problems. He wasn't sure whether they would, but he didn't know how else to punish them. Whipping them was not the answer, as all of the men were needed to help with planting, tending crops, and gathering food.

William hoped that another supply ship would arrive at Plymouth before winter. Because he had no way of being sure of that, the colony needed to store up as much extra food as possible. Once again, Squanto proved invaluable. He showed the men how to trap lobsters, gather mussels from the rocks along the seashore, catch eels in the brooks that ran into the bay by feeling for them in the mud with their feet, and recognize which berries and fruits were safe to eat.

The settlers had a problem with their food supply, however. The Indians were friendly—too friendly.

Just fifteen miles west was the Wampanoag village of Nemasket, and people from the village often walked to the Plymouth settlement to see what was going on. Once they arrived, they expected to be fed and entertained. While it was good to be neighborly, William realized that something had to change before the Indians ate their way through the community's food supply before winter. But solving the problem required a delicate balance. William did not wish to insult the Indians from Nemasket or make them feel unwelcome. After consulting with Isaac Allerton and Edward Winslow, it was decided that a diplomatic visit would be made to Massasoit to ask him to curb the constant flow of Indian visitors. They agreed to send along to the chief a copper chain with instructions that he should give it to anyone he wanted to visit Plymouth as a signal that he was Massasoit's messenger. Other Indians would not be welcome, at least until the settlers had built up their food supplies.

On July 2, Edward and Stephen set out on the diplomatic mission. They were accompanied by Squanto, who would guide them to Massasoit at Sowams, about forty miles to the southwest, and serve as their translator. They carried two gifts for the chief: the copper chain and a bright-red English hunting coat. Everyone, including William, waited anxiously for their safe return.

Meanwhile, under William's leadership the colonists at Plymouth kept busy tending their crops, catching eels, herring, and cod in the brooks and bay, picking berries, and hunting birds. The cornstalks were growing tall, with each plant bearing many ears of corn. The beans and squash twined among them were almost ready to pick.

Five days after setting out, on July 7, Edward and Stephen stumbled back into the settlement. They were weak from hunger. William watched them devour the food brought to them. When they had eaten, they told William how they'd had only a few small fish since leaving Plymouth. That appeared to be all that Massasoit and the Pokanokets at Sowams had to share. William was surprised. He'd imagined that the chief would always have ample food supplies on hand. Edward explained what he'd learned. The Indians saw the supply of food a little differently than the Englishmen did. Instead of storing up quantities of food, they would travel from place to place to feed off the available food sources and then move on when the season changed or a food source was exhausted. During winter their supply of stored food was meager, and they would go hungry for days at a time to stretch out what food they had. William wondered if this was partly the reason so many Indians from Nemasket liked coming to Plymouth and eating their food.

Despite returning hungry, Edward and Stephen reported their mission a success. Massasoit understood their predicament and accepted the copper chain. He promised to give it to anyone he sent on official business to the colony and to tell the other Indians in the Wampanoag confederation to stop visiting unless they had pelts they wanted to trade. Edward and Stephen also explained that Massasoit had sent Squanto to the Wampanoag villages to tell them about the new arrangements with their English neighbors.

William was glad to hear that Squanto had been given the role of finding them trading partners. Hopefully a brisk trade in beaver pelts would develop, and by the time the next ship arrived from England, the colonists would have a fine cargo to send back on the return voyage to help pay off their financial obligation to the Merchant Adventurers.

William was also pleased with another piece of information Edward Winslow relayed. On their way to and from Sowams, they had not been threatened by any of the Indians they passed on the trail. It appeared that Massasoit had been true to his word regarding the peace treaty he had agreed to with the colonists.

Soon after the two men made it safely back from visiting Massasoit, another one of the colonists faced danger. This time it was sixteen-year-old John Billington Jr. William shook his head when he heard the news. The young man had wandered off toward the south and not returned by nightfall. Maybe he was lost or had been captured. Either way, William had to decide what the community should do about it.

Chapter 10

Celebration

There was no point in sending out a search party to find John Billington Jr. No one knew the terrain well enough to lead such an expedition. When Squanto returned to Plymouth, William sent him back to Massasoit to ask if he'd heard anything about a lost European boy.

Squanto returned two weeks later with the news that John was in the hands of the Nauset tribe on Cape Cod. William was not happy to hear this. One of the Stranger families, the Billingtons had been nothing but trouble to the small colony, yet William felt he had to do his best to get John back safely. This meant sending a rescue party to meet with the tribe the colonists had stolen corn from on Cape Cod. William wondered how much of a grudge the tribe might bear.

After volunteering for the mission himself, William asked for nine others to go with him. The men, including Squanto and Tokamahamon, an Indian whom Massasoit had sent back to Plymouth with Squanto, climbed into the shallop and sailed off in hopes of retrieving John.

The men followed the shore of Cape Cod but soon ran into a storm and were forced to take shelter in a bay that Tokamahamon told them was called Cummaquid. In the shelter of the bay they saw several Indians collecting lobsters. Squanto and Tokamahamon went to talk with them and soon brought Iyanough, chief of the local tribe, to meet the colonists at the boat. The group spent the night at Iyanough's village, and the following morning the chief and several of his men accompanied them twenty miles east.

As they sailed along, William was amazed at how many Indians he saw onshore. There had seemed to be so few when they explored the area during November and December after their arrival at Cape Cod harbor. William's heart skipped a beat when Iyanough guided them to the same beach where the Indians had launched their attack against them on their way to discover Thievish Harbor.

William wasn't the only one who felt fearful as the shallop came close to shore and a large crowd of Indians began to approach. Taking up their muskets, the men ordered the Indians to stand back and approach the boat two at a time. One of the first two Indians to approach was the man whose seed corn the colonists had taken. He was not happy with them. With Squanto interpreting, William told the man they were sorry for their actions and promised to make the matter good by supplying him with more corn. The man seemed happy with this outcome. William felt good about it too. The colonists had never intended to steal the corn. They had planned to return with goods in exchange for it, but they never did. Now the matter had been set right.

Soon afterward Aspinet, chief of the Nauset tribe, approached. One of his men had John with him. The chief and his warriors laid down their bows and arrows onshore and waded out to the shallop, where they handed over the boy. In return William presented Aspinet with a knife. William and the chief talked together, using Squanto as their translator. Before the group left, peace was declared between the Plymouth colonists and the Nausets.

John seemed to have survived his ordeal unscathed. On the way back to Plymouth he explained how he'd wandered away from the settlement and gotten lost. He had roamed the wilderness for five days, surviving on nuts, roots, and berries before stumbling into a Manomet village. The chief of the Manomets had handed him on to the Nausets of Cape Cod. The Nausets had treated him well, though he was glad to have been rescued and to be on his way home.

The relief of getting John back in one piece was overshadowed, however, by some disturbing news. At their meeting Aspinet had told William that the Narragansett Indians had taken Massasoit captive and killed several of his men. William knew this could spell disaster for Plymouth Colony. The settlers had agreed to make Massasoit's enemies their enemies. Did this mean they were now at war with the Narragansetts? And if so, had the Narragansetts already gone on the offensive and attacked the colony? Half the men of Plymouth were with them on the rescue mission, making the settlement an easy target. William knew that all they could do at that moment was get home as quickly as possible. But once again, weather proved their enemy, slowing progress and forcing them to seek shelter ashore. To make matters worse, their supply of freshwater was running low, and the only water they could find ashore was brackish.

At the first break in the weather, the shallop headed for Plymouth, sailing as fast as it would go. The men arrived home safely though very thirsty. Thankfully everyone was alive and well at Plymouth, but William realized he needed to get to the bottom of the rumors of Massasoit's capture.

On August 12, 1621, William sent Squanto and Tokamahamon off to investigate. The next day one of Massasoit's warriors, Hobbamock, ran into Plymouth and breathlessly asked to speak to William. Using a few words of English and sign language, Hobbamock explained that Corbitant, a lesser chief, was trying to use the situation to win over the loyalty of the Indians at Nemasket. When Hobbamock had last seen Squanto, one of Corbitant's men was holding a knife to Squanto's throat and threatening to kill him because of his relationship with the colonists at Plymouth. Hobbamock indicated that Squanto was probably dead by now.

William immediately called Myles Standish, Edward Winslow, Stephen Hopkins, Isaac Allerton, and William Brewster together. The meeting was tense, as the action they took next could well determine whether they all lived or died. The group decided they must act decisively. Myles would lead a party of armed men to Nemasket and confront Corbitant. If Squanto was indeed dead, the colonists agreed that Myles should execute Corbitant. The armed group, accompanied by Hobbamock, who was a *pniese*, a warrior of special abilities and stamina, set out the following morning.

William did not go on the raid. As he waited anxiously at Plymouth for word of how the group had fared at Nemasket, the routine of tending the crops and continuing to build cottages continued. Thanks to the woodworking skill of John Alden, the new cottages being erected were built of wooden planks, or clapboard. The buildings were much more durable in New England's weather than the earlier structures that were built using wattle and daub.

Two days later the armed patrol arrived back at Plymouth accompanied by Squanto and Tokamahamon. The group had two wounded Indians with them.

Once he had eaten, Myles visited William to give a report. He explained how they had ventured off the track about three miles before Nemasket and hidden in the woods. After dark they made their way to the village, where Hobbamock led them to the *wetu*, or Indian dwelling, in which Corbitant had been staying. They surrounded the wetu, and several armed colonists burst inside. With Hobbamock as their translator they demanded to know where Corbitant was. Two men who tried to flee were both shot in the leg by the colonists outside. They were the two brought back to Plymouth. Samuel Fuller, the community's self-taught surgeon, was tending their wounds.

Myles told William they learned that Corbitant and his men had left the day before and no one knew where they were. Corbitant's warrior had not killed Squanto, who, along with Tokamahamon, was soon located. Before leaving Nemasket, Myles told the Indians they were not to listen to or support Corbitant should he return. The colonists were at peace with Massasoit and the Wampanoag and were duty-bound to take action against anyone who threatened that peace. The residents of Nemasket were afraid when they heard this, and Myles believed that they would not cause anymore trouble. William certainly hoped not.

Over the next several weeks, word filtered back to William of the effect of the night raid on Nemasket. Massasoit, who had indeed been taken prisoner by the Narragansetts, was released and returned to Sowams. A number of chiefs throughout the region sent congratulations to Governor Bradford. Even Corbitant sent a message that he wanted to make peace with the settlers. Seeing that the colonists would use force to honor their peace treaty with Massasoit brought a new calm among the Indian tribes. William was even more delighted when, on September 13, 1621, nine chiefs arrived at Plymouth to sign a treaty with the colonists and profess their loyalty to King James of England.

On Tuesday, September 18, Myles, accompanied by Squanto and several other men, climbed into the shallop and headed north. They were on their way to befriend the Massachusetts tribe and set up a trade arrangement for beaver pelts. William knew that the next supply ship that came to Plymouth needed to return to England with its hold filled with furs and oak clapboards to begin paying off the colonists' debt to the Merchant Adventurers. He ordered several men to saw clapboards while the others were away in the shallop.

When the group arrived back in Plymouth, the shallop was laden with soft beaver pelts. Myles reported that the Indians had many more and would trade with the colonists for them. The men who returned from the trading trip talked incessantly about the mighty bay and harbor they had encountered to their north. It was a deep harbor where ships of any size could come almost to the edge of the land, and there were two large rivers that boats could navigate into the interior. Where the two rivers converged at the bay, there was high ground that was easily defensible. The men's talk produced a sense of unease in the community. If only they had explored a little farther north, things might have been different. William told them that Providence had brought them to Plymouth. He reminded them that it was God who assigned men the "boundaries of their habitations." God had led them to Plymouth, and here they would stay and rejoice in His chosen dwelling place.

Meanwhile fall was upon them. The leaves on the trees around Plymouth turned vibrant shades of red, yellow, and orange. The amazing display was more vivid than any fall change William had experienced in England or Holland. By now the colonists had harvested their crops. The corn had been plentiful, as had the beans and squash. The leeks and onions they planted had also done well. But the barley and pea crops were not up to the standard William had hoped for. Some of the corn was dried and ground into meal, from which the women of the community would make corn cakes in the same way Squanto said the Indians did.

The colonists had worked hard all through the previous winter, spring, and summer. Many of the men had risked their lives to make peace with their Indian neighbors. John Billington Jr. had been rescued, and not a single person in the community had died since John and Catherine Carver in the spring. It was time to celebrate. William thought back to Leyden, where every October the Dutch took a day to celebrate gaining their freedom from the Spanish. He also remembered the festivals held in England to celebrate the harvest, where villagers gathered to feast, drink, and play games. William decided to combine these two festivals in the New World and called for three days of celebration. He invited Massasoit to join them and ordered several of the men to hunt wild turkeys and the ducks and geese that flew south in large flocks. Other men were sent to gather seafood: cod and lobsters and mussels from the bay.

Everyone in the community busied themselves preparing for the celebration, and William was delighted that this pulled the people all together. As the day for the start of the celebration approached in early October, Massasoit and ninety of his men arrived at Plymouth with five freshly killed deer. What furniture was available from the cottages was brought out for people to sit on and to serve food from. People sat on the chairs or the ground around a large fire over which the deer, ducks, geese, and turkeys were being roasted on spits and where several large pots of stew simmered. The children played while Indian braves demonstrated their accuracy with bows and arrows. The men of the community did the same with their muskets. When the game roasting over the fire had cooked, everyone ate until they were full. At night the Indians slept by the fire and the colonists in their cottages.

William had to admit it was quite a celebration, and an air of happiness and contentment seemed to hang over Plymouth. The colonists had arrived in the New World almost eleven months before. Things had been difficult. They had seen many deaths and had endured many hardships and trials, but they had survived. They had made peace with the Indians, who were now their allies. And they had planted themselves in the New World. They still had much work to do in building and establishing Plymouth, but they now had food supplies laid up for winter. Most important for William was that he believed they were in the place to which God had guided them. For that he was deeply thankful.

When the feasting and celebrating ended and Massasoit and his entourage returned to Sowams, it was time to prepare the settlement for the long winter ahead. William prayed that this time they would all survive it.

Chapter 11

The Challenge

Boom! went the cannon on top of The Mount on a crisp fall day in mid-November. William, who was in the fields with many of the other men, raced back toward the settlement. The cannon was to be fired only in an emergency.

"A ship is at the mouth of Plymouth Harbor," Myles yelled from the bottom of the hill. "Every man to his musket!"

William ran into his house, got his gun, and was soon assembled with all the men and boys, along with Squanto and Hobbamock. They stood shoulder to shoulder, muskets loaded, ready to fire. They gazed out at the small ship, about one-third the size of the *Mayflower*, that was sailing into the harbor. William squinted against the sun. Was the vessel flying a French flag? If it was, he was certain they would be needing their muskets. French privateers would not hesitate to plunder a poorly protected English village in the New World.

All eyes were on the ship, and a cheer went up when they could see the flag: a red cross on a white background, the cross of Saint George. This was an English ship. Was it a vessel that had been blown off course, as the *Mayflower* had been, or was it sent by the Merchant Adventurers? If it was the latter, William wondered who might be aboard. His heart quickened at the possibility that his son John, Pastor John Robinson, or even a group of eligible young women to take the place of the wives who had died during the past winter would be aboard. It was another two hours before he would find out.

The ship was anchored well out in Plymouth Bay, and the vessel's longboat came ashore. William learned that the ship, which carried thirty-six passengers, was the *Fortune* and had indeed been sent by the Merchant Adventurers. One of the first to come ashore from the longboat was Martha Ford, who was in labor. Martha arrived on the beach just in time to deliver a son, whom she named John. She was accompanied by her two-year-old daughter and a sick husband.

Several happy reunions took place as the passengers were brought ashore in the longboat. The Brewsters' oldest son Jonathan was aboard, as was Edward Winslow's brother John. Robert Cushman and his fourteen-year-old son Thomas were also on the *Fortune*. But neither John Bradford nor John Robinson was among the passengers.

William was dismayed to see that most of the passengers were young men and almost all were Strangers. Besides Martha Ford and her daughter, only one other female was aboard. William quickly calculated that the colony would now be made up of sixty-six men and boys and just sixteen women, not a good balance. Worse, the extra thirty-three males would undoubtedly be hearty eaters, and no extra food supplies had been sent on the ship.

William found the situation impossible to fathom. How could Thomas Weston of the Merchant Adventurers have sent thirty-six people to Plymouth with winter ahead and not send extra provisions to feed them? William thought grimly that nearly doubling the number of colonists at Plymouth could mean only one thing: food rations for the winter would have to be halved. This was not something he looked forward to announcing, but he could not see how the current supply of corn and other food commodities the community had worked hard to store up would last all winter without reducing the rations. Even as the settlers helped passengers out of the *Fortune*'s longboat, William could see the way many of them looked warily at the newcomers. He knew they too were wondering how they were all going to get along.

The first test was housing. By now Plymouth had eleven cottages and four common buildings. The thirty-six passengers and newborn baby from the *Fortune* had to be distributed among the already crowded dwellings. William ordered every family to take two of the male arrivals to live with them, while the rest would be accommodated in the common house until more cottages could be built.

As unbelievable as it seemed to William, most of the passengers had not even thought to bring warm bedding or cooking pots or anything of practical value. A few chickens were on board the ship. William hoped they would provide some eggs for the group.

That evening, Robert Cushman handed a land patent document to William. The document was issued by the Council for New England, a body that had been formed the year before. Much like the Virginia Company of London, the Council for New England was responsible for establishing settlements in New England. The patent stated that the Council recognized the Mayflower Compact and that after seven years each settler would be awarded one hundred acres of land. This was good news for William. The residents of Plymouth now had a legal right to the land they had settled.

Robert also handed William a letter addressed to Governor John Carver, now dead. As he read the letter, William's delight at receiving the land patent turned to anger. The letter was from Thomas Weston, who wrote that he was upset that the *Mayflower* had returned to England empty and that the colonists had kept the ship anchored for so long. Thomas accused Governor Carver and the colonists of not doing enough to secure a return on the Merchant Adventurers' investment. He also chastised John for weakness of judgment, saying there was too much talk and not enough action among the men in the colony.

Why, he asked, hadn't he made sure the *Mayflower* returned to England with its hold full of goods to be sold for profit? Thomas was also upset that the Separatist men had not signed the amended contract with the Merchant Adventurers, which was presented to them at Southampton in England. He concluded his letter by demanding that they sign it now. Then he threatened that many of the Merchant Adventurers might withdraw their backing for the venture unless the colonists improved their performance.

William was furious. He understood that the Merchant Adventurers deserved a return on their investment and that the colonists had done nothing to repay them. But for Thomas Weston to sit in his comfortable house in London and criticize them for all of this was an outrage. Thomas had no idea what the colonists had been through as they exhausted every ounce of their strength to survive. As for Governor John Carver, he had worked himself to death for the survival of the colony.

After his anger subsided, William sat down and carefully crafted a letter to Thomas Weston, explaining just how unhelpful it was to get discouraging news from him. He began writing,

You greatly blame us for keeping the ship here so long in the countrie, and then to send her away emptie. She lay five weeks at Cap-Codd, whilst with many a weary step (after a long journey) and enduring many a hard brunte, we sought out in the foule winter a place of habitation. Then we went in so tedious a

time to make provission of sheelter for us
and our goods, aboute which labour, many
of our armes and legs can tell us to this day
we were not necligent. But it pleased God to
vissite us then, with death dayly, and with so
general a disease, that the living were scarce
able to burie the dead; and the well not in any
measure sufficiente to tend to the sick. And
now to be so greatly blamed, for not freighting
[loading] the ship [with goods], doth indeed
goe near us, and much discourages us.

Once he had said everything he wanted to say to
Thomas Weston, William felt better. However, at
the urging of Robert Cushman, William did follow
through on one of Thomas's demands and had the
Separatist men sign the amended contract they had
refused to sign back in Southampton.

To help set the record straight about the colony
and hopefully to attract new settlers to Plymouth,
William and Edward wrote a manuscript detailing
the first thirteen months of the colony's history. Of
course, since they wanted to attract new settlers,
they had played down descriptions of the sickness
and death that had nearly doomed the settlement in
its first months. The manuscript was wrapped in a
large sheet of parchment to be sent back to England
on the *Fortune* for publication. Robert already had
someone in mind who he thought would be willing
to publish it.

Unlike Captain Christopher Jones of the *Mayflower*, the captain of the *Fortune* wanted to be on

his way back to England as soon as possible. The colonists busied themselves loading the ship with the beaver and otter pelts they had traded from the Indians, along with oak clapboards and sassafras. All in all, William and Robert calculated the value of the cargo to be about five hundred pounds in England, half the amount they owed the Merchant Adventurers. William looked forward to the day that the debt was paid back completely.

While the ship was being loaded, the settlers paused for two funerals. Martha Ford's newborn son had died, as had Martha's ailing husband. William prayed that it was not the beginning of another dark winter of death.

On Wednesday, December 12, 1621, the captain of the *Fortune* announced that he would be sailing on the following morning's tide. Robert decided to return to England with the ship. That way he could hand deliver the contract the men had signed, along with William's letter to Thomas Weston, and see that the manuscript got into the right hands. He asked William if his fourteen-year-old son could stay in Plymouth. William agreed to take responsibility for him.

One other important piece of paper was leaving on the *Fortune*: a letter addressed to Alice Southworth. One of the arriving passengers on the *Fortune* was William Wright, an Englishman from the Leyden congregation. He'd told William that Alice, another member of the congregation, had recently become a widow and was raising two young boys alone. William remembered Alice well and began to pray about the possibility of asking her to join him in Plymouth. He felt that God blessed the idea, and he wrote a letter asking her to come to the New World and become his wife.

Once the *Fortune* sailed, William faced the reality of feeding, clothing, and governing a community that had instantly nearly doubled in size. Food rations were cut in half, any extra bedding the original colonists had was handed over to the new arrivals, or Newcomers, as they were already being dubbed, and plans began for the erecting of more dwellings in Plymouth.

While William dealt with integrating the Newcomers into the community and handling the squabbles that arose over who would live where, a messenger from the Narragansett tribe arrived in the settlement and asked for Squanto. Since Squanto was away from Plymouth at the time, the messenger left the parcel he carried for Squanto's return. It was a bundle of arrows wrapped in a rattlesnake skin. As they studied the package, William and Edward imagined that it was a challenge from the Narragansett chief, Canonicus, but they waited for Squanto to get back to be sure.

Squanto shook his head when William showed him what the messenger had left. "Canonicus is jealous that you have aligned yourselves with the Pokanokets. They are his enemy. You are right, this is indeed a challenge to war."

William knew he needed to act decisively, and fast. He asked Myles to bring him some gunpowder and musket balls, which he placed in the rattlesnake skin and gave to Squanto for delivery to Canonicus. If the Narragansetts wanted war, the colonists would show no weakness. They would meet them head-on.

It was a good countermove in theory, but as he looked around Plymouth, William was struck by just how easy it would be for a war party to overrun the settlement. He had believed that the peace treaty with Massasoit would make the settlement immune from Indian attacks. Now he realized that they had not accounted for the fact that other, stronger tribes like the Narragansett, enemies of Massasoit and the Pokanokets, might choose to attack them. Now that the community had more men, the time had come to fortify Plymouth. Once again William called for Myles Standish, who had studied military strategy while living in Holland. The two men came up with a plan. They would completely encompass the settlement and The Mount with a ten-foot-high palisade made of pales, logs with pointed tips on top, set side by side in the ground.

When William and Myles paced out the length for the palisade, it came to twenty-seven hundred feet. Building such a fence was a daunting task, especially with winter coming, but William was convinced it was necessary for the community's safety. Before work could begin, however, several of the cottages needed to be expanded to make them more comfortable for the greater number of people living in them. This would be done by adding lean-tos onto the sides of the structures. Work began immediately on the project.

Christmas Day approached as expansion of the

cottages began. William realized that the original colonists had now been settled in Plymouth for a year. So much had been accomplished in that time under the most difficult circumstances, but much more remained to be done. As had occurred the year before, since the Separatists did not celebrate Christmas, William expected the whole community to work that day, but things were different this time. The Newcomers from the *Fortune* wanted to take the day off. William urged them to keep working, but many of them were adamant that it was against their conscience to work on such a holy day. In the end, William gave the Strangers Christmas Day off while the Separatists went into the woods to fell trees.

When the Separatist men returned to the settlement in the early afternoon, they found the Strangers partying in the street, drinking cups of beer and playing stool ball. William was furious. It was one thing to claim a religious holiday but quite another to spend the day drinking and playing. William confiscated the Strangers' bats and balls and told them to either get back to work or retire to their houses to pray and worship God quietly on their holy day. William realized just how difficult it was going to be to mold the group into a unit that could work together to repel enemy attacks and continue building their town, much less make it the religious haven he and the other Separatists had dreamed of.

After the job of adding lean-tos onto the cottages was complete, work began in mid-February 1622 on building the palisade. It was a huge but necessary task. The work was backbreaking, and William was now glad that the *Fortune* had brought so many young, able-bodied men. The forest around Plymouth soon reverberated with the sound of axes chopping down trees. Once a tree was felled, it needed to be trimmed of all its branches. Then the trunk was cut into a twelve-foot length, with the top end sharpened to a point to make a pale. Once a pale had been prepared, it was carried by several men back to Plymouth. William wished they had oxen or horses to pull the heavy loads, but they did not.

At Plymouth another group of men worked away digging a two-foot-deep trench around the perimeter of the settlement and The Mount. William wasn't sure which job was harder, felling trees and shaping pales or using picks to chip through the frozen topsoil to dig the trench. The pales were stood upright and their bottoms dropped into the trench. They had to be maneuvered together side by side as closely as possible, leaving no gaps that attacking Indians or even arrows might be able to squeeze through. Then the men put the soil back in the trench and tamped it down hard so that the pales stood upright and in place.

Surviving now on half food rations, even the strongest of the men faltered under the constant workload. Sometimes a man would be so weak he would stumble and collapse. William felt the gnaw of hunger in his own stomach and the weakness it brought. He wished he could increase the food ration for the workingmen, but the truth was, he had doubts about whether their food supply would last them through the winter, even on half rations.

All he could do as governor was praise and encourage the men for their great effort.

The men's effort paid off. By the end of March, the palisade was complete. Plymouth and The Mount were now ringed by a defensive wall. William had to admit that it wasn't the prettiest palisade. Sap dripped from the newly cut pales, and bark peeled from them, but given the few tools they had to work with and the physical condition of the men, he was deeply thankful for it. The palisade would surely lead to the permanence of Plymouth. It would no longer be so easy for an attacking Indian war party to wipe out the colony in one fell swoop.

Chapter 12

Hunger Was a Close Companion

On a spring day in 1622, Myles Standish stood at the doorway to the Brewsters' cottage, where William lived. "I think we have trouble brewing," he said. "Hobbamock wants to talk to both of us in private."

William raised his eyebrows. "What is this about?"

"I'm not sure. He says he wants us both to hear what he has to say at the same time so we can judge it together."

William walked to the door. "Well then, we must oblige him."

A few minutes later, the three men walked out of the newly built palisade and into an open field where no one could hear their conversation. As Hobbamock spoke, William was amazed at how much the Indian's grasp of English had improved by being around the settlement, though his accent was still strong and sometimes hard to understand.

"I have heard that the Massachusetts and the Narragansetts have joined together and are planning to attack the trading party you plan to send north to trade for furs. Then, with so many able-bodied men out of the way, they are going to attack the settlement," Hobbamock said.

William was shocked. "Are you sure?" he asked. "How would they know we are about to send out a trading party?"

Hobbamock looked at the ground. "There is someone here giving them information, someone who wants to stir up trouble and see you all dead."

"Who?" William asked.

"All winter, while you have been building this palisade, Squanto has been plotting this."

"Squanto? That's impossible!" William replied.

"Is it?" Hobbamock asked. "Have you seen how often he leaves the settlement?"

William thought back. Lately Squanto did seem to come and go a lot.

Later that night, William, Myles, William Brewster, Edward, and William's assistant Isaac Allerton met to discuss the situation. They all agreed it was impossible to know who to trust. Was Hobbamock telling the truth about Squanto, or was he setting Squanto up so that William would ban him from the settlement and Hobbamock could take his place as the most important Indian at Plymouth? In the end the group decided to proceed as if nothing had happened and to wait and see what might occur when the trading party left for the Massachusetts.

In April the shallop left Plymouth on the trading mission. Onboard were Myles Standish and twelve men from the community, including Squanto and Hobbamock. No one told Squanto that he was under suspicion, nor did anyone else in the settlement, except William and his inner circle of advisors, know about the situation.

Several hours after the shallop had sailed away, there was a commotion at the settlement gate. William hurried over to see what was going on. In front of him stood an Indian man, blood dripping from a wound on his head. He yelled, "I have come from Nemasket. The Narragansetts and Massasoit's men are coming to attack you. Beware! Get your guns!" William recognized the man as a cousin of Squanto. "They beat me when I tried to tell them they should not do this," the Indian continued, "but I escaped to warn you."

By now a number of people were standing around William. "What should we do?" one of the men asked.

William wasn't sure. There was something odd about this man. Could he be giving a performance? Had Squanto put his cousin up to this immediately following the departure of thirteen men from the community? And if so, why would he do such a thing? Were Squanto and Hobbamock involved in some kind of power struggle? It was impossible to tell.

"Shoot the cannon," William ordered. "We need to get everyone inside the palisade."

One of the cannons on top of The Mount was fired, and a large boom reverberated across Plymouth Bay. Meanwhile the remaining men busied themselves loading their muskets and taking up defensive positions, just as Myles had taught them. When all those who had been outside the palisade returned, the gates were firmly shut, with Squanto's cousin also inside the settlement.

As night fell, Myles and the trading group arrived at the gate. William was surprised to see them. Myles explained that the wind had not been favorable and the shallop had only made it outside the entrance to Plymouth Bay when he heard the cannon fire. They turned around immediately and had managed to make it back to Plymouth. Soon Squanto, his cousin, and Hobbamock all met in William Brewster's cottage, along with Myles and William's other advisors. It was time to get to the bottom of the matter.

The meeting did not go well. Hobbamock accused Squanto of setting up the whole incident with his cousin to trick the colonists into believing that Massasoit was their enemy so they would attack the great chief and kill him. Then, according to Hobbamock, Squanto planned to take advantage of the confusion and name himself the new chief. It sounded preposterous, but was it true? The best way to find out, William decided, was to send someone to the Pokanokets to see if they were indeed planning an attack. Hobbamock's wife offered to go. She left early the next morning, with everyone anxiously awaiting her return. Had Massasoit betrayed them and was going to attack, or had Squanto been playing a giant game of chess, moving William and the people of Plymouth around like pawns?

Nearly three days passed before Hobbamock's wife returned to Plymouth with her observations. No, Massasoit and his men were not planning an attack on the settlement. But the chief had insisted she tell him why she was visiting. When Massasoit learned that Squanto had tried to turn the colonists against him, he was furious. He demanded that Hobbamock's wife tell William to send Squanto back to him so he could be properly punished.

For William this was a terrible mess. He was sure the punishment Massasoit would mete out to Squanto would be some kind of torturous death. And even though it appeared that Squanto had betrayed them, William could not bear to think of his friend and the translator he had come to rely upon being killed. Yet he knew that under the terms of the peace treaty with Massasoit he was obliged to turn over Squanto.

William wrestled with what to do. He decided to do nothing for the time being and to wait and see if something might distract Massasoit's attention. But Massasoit did not forget. The following month he arrived at Plymouth. The chief was enraged by Squanto's treachery and demanded that William turn him over. William did his best to try to pacify Massasoit by telling the chief that indeed Squanto deserved to die for what he had done. But he also insisted that Squanto's presence at Plymouth was essential if the community was to survive. Squanto was their main translator, and William and the community had come

to rely upon him. For this reason he was too important to be executed. Massasoit listened patiently, but
it was clear to William when Massasoit abruptly left
Plymouth that the chief did not accept these arguments. He wanted Squanto executed.

Two days after Massasoit left Plymouth, he sent
a messenger and several warriors back to the settlement. The warriors brought with them a quantity
of excellent beaver pelts, and the messenger carried
Massasoit's knife. William knew that this was the
traditional sign that the messenger spoke for the
chief. The messenger explained that the great chief
wanted the colonists to kill Squanto and send his
head and hands back with the messenger. The beaver pelts were payment from Massasoit for Squanto's life. William said he would not receive the pelts
as payment for a man, yet he knew he was bound
by the treaty between the colonists and the Wampanoags. Was he willing to let his friendship with
Squanto sever his already-strained relations with
Massasoit? Was he willing to put the future of Plymouth on the line for a man—a man who appeared to
have acted treacherously toward both the colonists
and Massasoit?

Despite the struggle with his conscience, William
knew he must turn over Squanto. He was just about
to do so when a call went out that a ship was at the
entrance to Plymouth Bay. With that, William told
Massasoit's messenger that he could not turn over
Squanto until the nationality of the vessel was deter-
mined. It might be a French privateer, in which case
Squanto would be needed to fight. The messenger

and the warriors stormed out of Plymouth, taking with them the beaver pelts they had brought.

The boat turned out to be a shallop. In it were seven men sent by Thomas Weston. The shallop was from the fishing boat hired to transport them across the Atlantic. The men carried with them several letters from Thomas and one from Robert Cushman. William could scarcely believe the news the letters contained. Thomas wrote, "I find ye general so backward and your friends in Leyden so cold that I fear you must stand on your own legs and trust (as they say) to God and yourselves." The colonists at Plymouth could expect no more support or supplies from the Merchant Adventurers. William realized that since the Separatists had left England twenty months before, Thomas and the Merchant Adventurers had provided the colonists with no support and no supplies. All the investors had done was send more unprepared settlers to Plymouth to burden the already-burdened community. While it was daunting to be told to expect no more support, William knew that he and the other colonists would have to continue finding their own way to survive, as they had done since first arriving in the New World.

Thomas went on to explain that he had secured a land patent in New England where he was going to establish his own colony. The seven men who had arrived on the shallop were the first batch of people who would found it. As such they did not fall under the authority of the colonists at Plymouth. Nonetheless, Thomas wrote that he expected the colonists to feed and house the men and those who would arrive on two more ships, and to provide them with whatever was needed as they went about establishing their settlement.

William was dumbfounded. The residents of Plymouth were practically starving. The abundant flocks of ducks and geese that flew overhead the previous spring were scarce this spring, and the men were having a hard time shooting them. And while the bay contained an abundant supply of fish such as cod, bluefish, and striped bass, most of the colonists had been farmers back in England, not fishermen. They did not have the knack or the necessary equipment, such as nets and sturdy fishing lines, for catching large quantities of fish. The nets they made at Plymouth proved too weak under the weight of fish and would burst open when they tried to haul them in. Instead, the men had taken to searching for shellfish in the mudflats around Plymouth at low tide. Their corn was planted, but the shoots were scarcely out of the ground, and there were many months to go before it would be ready to harvest. In the meantime, the colonists were trying to survive on the meager food supplies they still had and on what they could scrounge from the bay and surrounding forest. Despite their best efforts, hunger was a close companion.

The letter from Robert Cushman also had crushing news for William. Before the *Fortune* reached England, the vessel had been intercepted by a French privateer. The pirates had stolen the entire cargo the colonists were sending back to help pay off their debt to the Merchant Adventurers. The one bright spot in the letter was the news that the French pirates, while stripping the ship of almost everything, had overlooked the manuscript that William and Edward Winslow had written and Robert was now making plans to have published.

When he had finished reading the letters, William showed them to his closest advisors. The colonists were hungry and lonely. They did not need to know, at least not now, that they had been abandoned by the Merchant Adventurers.

Despite the tenuous food situation at Plymouth, William found space for the seven new arrivals and began supplying them with food rations, much to the chagrin of some members of the community.

In late June 1622, the situation got even worse. Two ships, the *Charity* and the *Swan*, carrying the remaining sixty men who would found Thomas Weston's new community, arrived in Plymouth Harbor. Expecting their arrival, William had ordered that several more shelters be built to temporarily house them. The first seven men had already scouted and negotiated with the Indians for land for their colony at Wessagusset, twenty-two miles north of Plymouth. Of course, the problem of feeding the new arrivals continued, and hunger was still ever present. The new arrivals were none too happy about the meager supply of food and took to stealing nearly ripened ears of corn from the fields.

Soon after the arrival of the men for the new colony, a longboat arrived at Plymouth to deliver news for William. The men in the boat said that cod fishing season was in full swing. Three or four hundred fishing boats that had crossed the Atlantic from England were gathered off the coast of New England, farther to the north, and were now busy catching fish. The fishing vessel the men had been on was now traveling north from Virginia to join in the cod fishing. The boat's captain, John Huddleston, had written a letter to the governor of Plymouth and had asked the men to deliver it.

In the letter, Captain Huddleston had written news from Jamestown. On March 22, 1622, Indians had attacked and killed 347 people there, one-fourth of Jamestown's population. The captain wanted those at Plymouth to be forewarned lest the same thing happen to them. William was stunned by the news. Indians had massacred over three times the population of Plymouth in one attack. It was a sobering thought, especially since relations with Massasoit were strained over the situation with Squanto. Perhaps even more frightening were the rumors that had recently seeped back to Plymouth that the Massachusetts and Narragansetts were planning an attack on the settlement.

Given this turn of events, William decided they needed to strengthen their fortifications at Plymouth. He ordered that a fort be built atop The Mount overlooking the settlement. It was to be a one-story structure of sturdy oak timber with a flat roof on which the cannons would be mounted. Work began immediately, but progress was slow because the men were weak from hunger.

William knew he had to do something about the dwindling food supply. He and Edward devised a plan. Perhaps the boats fishing for cod farther up the coast would supply them with some much-needed food. After all, Captain Huddleston had been concerned enough about the settlers and their survival to send a letter warning them to be wary of Indian attacks. Accompanied by several men, Edward set out in the shallop to find the fishing fleet.

While the men were away, Thomas Weston's men left Plymouth and moved to Wessagusset, where they began to build their own fort.

When he returned to Plymouth, Edward was happy to report that the captains of the fishing boats had been sympathetic to their needs and supplied them with what food supplies and fish they could spare. William calculated that the food Edward had returned with would allow him to increase the daily food ration by four ounces per day per person. He knew it wasn't much, but it was the best he could do. William posted a guard at the storehouse doors lest someone break in and steal the food.

When the corn was harvested, William was disappointed. It was smaller than the year before, much too small to put an end to the community's hunger. William blamed two things for the situation. First, the members of the community were so weakened from hunger they had not had the energy to tend to the growing corn crop as they had the year before. But mostly he blamed the men from the Wessagusset colony who had simply stolen the corn, with no thought for others or the future.

As it turned out, the men at the Wessagusset colony were even more desperate for food than the residents of Plymouth. As a result, in November, Richard Greene, the leader of the Wessagusset colony and also Thomas Weston's brother-in-law, approached William with a plan. While the *Charity* had returned to England after bringing the settlers for the new colony to Plymouth, the *Swan*, a thirty-ton vessel, had stayed behind to serve the colony. Richard suggested that the two colonies combine their efforts. Using the *Swan*, they could sail around Cape Cod and, drawing on the Plymouth colonists' experience, trade with various Indian tribes for food. William agreed to the plan, charging Myles to lead the expedition. When the time came for the *Swan* to depart Plymouth, however, Myles was ill, and William decided to go instead, taking Squanto along with him.

As they sailed away from Plymouth, William prayed that God would grant them favor with the Indians. Their situation was grim. They desperately needed more food. They sailed down the outside of Cape Cod to its elbow, where they encountered the same treacherous currents that had turned back the *Mayflower*. However, with Squanto's knowledge of the area, they were able to locate a narrow, winding channel that led them into a large bay, which Squanto told them was called Manamoyick. There they dropped anchor.

The next morning William and Squanto went ashore to talk to the local Indians. At first the locals seemed suspicious of them and hid their possessions. William and Squanto decided the Indians probably thought the two of them had come to plunder their wetus. Over the next several days, however, they established trust and developed friendly relations with the Manamoyicks. As a result, the colonists were able to secure eight hogsheads, equivalent to eight large barrels, of corn and beans. It was enough to stave off starvation, at least for the time being.

After loading the corn and beans aboard the *Swan*, the men prepared to set sail, hoping to find another tribe to trade with. But before they could sail, Squanto became ill. His nose bled profusely, and he had a high fever. As William did everything possible to care for his ailing friend, Squanto asked him to pray for him so that if he died he would go to be with the Englishmen's God in heaven. Squanto's condition continued to worsen, and two days later he was dead. For William this was another blow, another personal loss like the death of his wife, Dorothy. Squanto and William had developed a deep friendship that had not weakened, despite Squanto's treachery in plotting against Massasoit. Once more William felt the bite of loneliness in the New World. He was sure that Squanto had been a gift from God. Without him, the colonists at Plymouth would probably not have survived their first year.

Without a translator, William decided that the *Swan* should return to Plymouth. As they sailed back, William realized that the settlement must now rely on Hobbamock as their translator and guide. But while Hobbamock's English continued to improve, he had never lived in England as Squanto had, and he did not have the same depth of understanding of Englishmen and their ways. It was now the beginning of December, less than a month before a new year would be upon them. William hoped and prayed that 1623 would be less trying to both body and soul than 1622 had been.

Chapter 13

"I Will Never Forget This Kindness"

In February 1623, William received a letter from John Sanders, the new leader of the settlement at Wessagusset who had taken over when Richard Greene died. The letter explained that things were desperate at Wessagusset. The men there had quickly eaten all the corn and beans acquired on the *Swan's* trading expedition. They had taken to selling their clothes and blankets in exchange for food from the Indians and had even stolen food from them. Several men had already died from starvation. As a result, the settlers at Wessagusset wanted to launch an attack on the local Indians and capture their food supply. But before engaging in such an attack, John wanted to know what William thought of the plan.

William thought it was a terrible idea and immediately wrote back to John telling him so. He explained that such an attack would lead to retaliation, and not just against the men at Wessagusset but most likely against the colonists at Plymouth as well. Instead, he encouraged the men to do what the residents of Plymouth were having to do—forage along the seashore for mussels and clams and dig up edible roots, or ground nuts, as they were calling them. William noted that it was possible but not necessarily pleasant to live off these limited foods, and he hoped that the Wessagusset colonists would heed his advice.

The following month news reached Plymouth that Massasoit was ill and may well die. The news distressed William. Even though his relationship with Massasoit was strained over the refusal to hand over Squanto, the chief was still their main ally. Massasoit had asked for Edward Winslow to visit him at Sowams. William ordered Edward to set out immediately. Edward quickly gathered some medicine and a supply of food and before nightfall was on his way to visit the chief, accompanied by John Hamden and Hobbamock.

A week passed before Edward arrived back at Plymouth bringing good news. Massasoit was making a steady recovery from his illness. Edward told William that when he arrived at Sowams, the chief was very weak, having not eaten for several days. Everyone in the village, even the medicine man, seemed resigned to the chief's impending death. But Edward gave Massasoit a dose of medicine and coaxed him to eat by spreading some fruit jam on his tongue. The chief finally swallowed it, and little by little his strength began to return.

Edward continued giving Massasoit doses of medicine and made him duck soup with cornmeal in it, which the chief ate. Soon Massasoit was strong enough to sit up and begin eating more solid food. Edward explained how the chief continually thanked him for making him well. And with a twinkle in his eye, he recounted Massasoit's exact words: "Now I see the English are my friends and love me. While I live, I will never forget this kindness they have showed me." William was elated. Thanks to Edward, the strained relationship with Massasoit was now back on solid ground.

"There is one more thing," Edward said. "As a parting gift, Massasoit passed on to me some disturbing news. The Indians know that Weston's men are planning an attack on them, and they are planning their own attack on Wessagusset and on Plymouth. They see us as one people. Massasoit wants us to kill those Massachusetts Indians before they kill us."

The news was disturbing, and William knew something needed to be done about the situation. Should they follow Massasoit's urging and kill those Massachusetts plotting against them? Would that calm matters down or make things worse? William did not know, and it was not a decision he wanted to make alone. On March 23, 1623, he convened a community meeting at which he revealed the Massachusetts' plot to attack them and asked the community whether they would give their consent to a preemptive attack. After some debate, the residents of Plymouth felt that William should be the one to make that decision.

William consulted with Myles Standish, and the two came up with a plan. Myles would take eight men with him and go to Wessagusset. Once there, they would kill the Indian leaders of the planned attack, whom Myles had learned were two sub-chiefs, Wituwamat and Pecksuot. Before the group set out, William ordered them to return to Plymouth with Wituwamat's head as a reminder of what would become of other Indians who thought about attacking English colonists.

Once again William found himself waiting anxiously at Plymouth for news. With the first sight of the shallop in the bay, he rushed down to the water's edge to meet them. One glance told him what he wanted to know. In the bottom of the boat was a bloodstained parcel of linen containing Wituwamat's severed head. Myles reported that their mission had been a success. They had killed not only Wituwamat and Pecksuot but also Wituwamat's eighteen-year-old brother and another brave. Following that, there was a skirmish with braves from the Massachusetts tribe in which three more Indians were killed before the braves fled. Myles was sure there would be no more trouble from the Massachusetts tribe. He also reported that the Englishmen at Wessagusset had abandoned their settlement. Some had gone farther up the New England coast, but most had decided to return to England. William was glad to hear it.

Thomas Weston's colony had been nothing but trouble since the day the men had arrived in Plymouth.

Two weeks after the attack on the Massachusetts at Wessagusset, William Bradford stood dumbfounded. He could hardly believe his eyes as he looked at the bedraggled, half-naked Englishman who had walked into Plymouth and asked to speak with him. The man was Thomas Weston himself! William had not seen him since Southampton before the *Mayflower* and the *Speedwell* set sail from there nearly three years ago.

Thomas, who was now no longer associated with the Merchant Adventurers, explained that he'd come to New England and was on his way down the coast to visit his colony at Wessagusset when his boat was wrecked. He survived the wreck and was washed up on the shore, only to be captured by Indians. They took everything he had managed to save from the sinking ship, even most of his clothes. He was sure they were going to kill him, but somehow he had managed to escape. He set out walking south, and once he learned that his colony at Wessagusset had already been abandoned, he walked on to Plymouth.

William could hardly believe that Thomas was in Plymouth asking for his help. After all, he'd lorded it over the Separatists, being rude and insolent to them and their beliefs. Even from across the Atlantic Ocean he had made the colonists' lives difficult through his unwillingness to send them supplies. Now here he was, standing before William, barely clothed and penniless. While it would have been easy to gloat, William realized that here was another

Englishman who, regardless of his past actions, was in desperate need. The Bible said to feed the hungry and clothe the naked, and William knew that was what he must do.

Once he had eaten and slept, Thomas asked William if the colony would loan him some beaver pelts that he could use for trade. In exchange he said that a supply ship was on its way from England. When it arrived, they could have anything from the ship's cargo they wanted. William was doubtful. He'd heard Thomas make many promises, only to break them. Despite his feelings about the man, William recognized that Thomas was the person who had organized and paid for the Separatists to get from England to the New World. Because of this, William and several of his advisors privately decided to loan him 170 pounds of pelts.

Sure enough, repaying his debt to William and the leaders of Plymouth was another one of Thomas's empty promises. Thomas disappeared from the settlement, taking the pelts with him, and was never seen again in Plymouth. William was not surprised that neither did a supply ship arrive. He had dealt with Thomas long enough to expect that this would be the outcome. But as a Christian, he felt he'd been obedient to God by helping a man in need.

Now that it was spring, William turned his attention to getting crops planted. Food remained in short supply, and he knew that this year they must ensure a good harvest. If they didn't have one, they might not otherwise survive the next winter. As planting season approached, William decided to make some changes. The agreement the Plymouth colonists had signed with the Merchant Adventurers required them to work for the general good of the community and not for themselves. This approach had its problems and had bred discontent. Some of the unmarried men were not happy that they were working for everyone, including other men's wives and children. Some of the women objected to cooking and washing for the unmarried men. And of course, those who worked hard at tending the crops and gathering food supplies were getting the same rations as those who were lazy. William consulted with his advisors and then decided to break the agreement with the Merchant Adventurers. He would assign a plot of land to each household in the community according to its size. The members of the household would plant, tend, and raise their own corn and other crops on their plot.

The change was enthusiastically embraced by the residents of Plymouth, who were soon busy catching herring in the brook and planting their corn and beans and squash in the manner Squanto had shown them. For William it was a joy for once to see men, women, and children gladly tending their crops. He also noticed that much more corn was planted than the year before.

Of course, between planting their crops and harvesting them several months later, the colonists needed to feed themselves. Like everyone else in the colony, there were some nights William went to bed not knowing what he would eat the next day, perhaps some ground nuts, perhaps some mussels and clams foraged along the seashore. The situation was made worse by the fact that the Indians were reluctant to trade any food or pelts with them. Hobbamock explained that because of the killings at Wessagusset they were fearful of visiting Plymouth to trade.

The residents of Plymouth continued foraging for food along the seashore and in the forest. Occasionally a man would shoot a deer whose meat was shared with everyone, but this was never quite enough to stave off the constant hunger. And although their fishing skills were not good, William divided the men of the community into groups of six. He set up a schedule whereby a group would go out onto the bay in the shallop to fish, with instructions not to return until they had caught something. When one group returned, another group would take the shallop out to fish so that there was always a group out fishing. Sometimes a group would stay out fishing all night because they had caught nothing during the day.

William was happy when he saw the shoots of corn begin to break out of the ground. It looked to him to be a bountiful crop on the way. A problem soon arose, though. The gentle rain that normally fell this time of year did not come. Each day William looked at the sky with concern. No clouds were to be seen, just clear blue sky with the sun burning down. With each passing hot, clear day, the young corn stalks drooped and dried out. By mid-July it seemed that the crop would be destroyed because of the lack of water.

As he looked out at the wilting corn crop, William began to wonder whether this was some kind of punishment from God for something they had done or, perhaps, failed to do. He decided to call the whole community together for what he called a "solemn day of humiliation" during which they would fast and pray. The whole community, both Separatists and Strangers, gathered in the fort on The Mount, which was also used as a community meeting hall. William ordered the doors shut, and everyone began to pray, asking God to send rain and save their crops and give them a bountiful harvest. Eight hours later, when they opened the doors the weather had turned overcast. By the following morning, rain was falling. William prayed a heartfelt thanks to God.

Gentle rain continued to fall for the next two weeks. Everyone watched in amazement as the parched corn stalks that many had given up for dead burst back to life. The stalks turned a vibrant green and began to shoot out an abundance of ears of corn. William was relieved. It seemed that they were going to have a bountiful harvest after all. William was doubly relieved when Myles Standish returned to Plymouth with provisions he'd been able to trade from tribes farther along the coast.

In early August, as William looked out across Plymouth Bay, he watched a ship sail up and drop anchor. The vessel was the *Anne*, and William soon learned that it was the first of two ships sent out by the Merchant Adventurers. Not only was the *Anne* carrying about sixty passengers, but it also had supplies for the colony stored in its hold, including a number of pigs and goats to be used for breeding.

The whole of the Plymouth community gathered on the seashore as the *Anne's* longboat began ferrying passengers ashore. William, like the other Separatists, watched hopefully to see who from Leyden might be aboard. The Brewsters' daughters, Patience and Fear, were aboard, as were the wife and five daughters of Richard Warren, one of the Strangers. Shouts of joy filled the air, and tears rolled down faces as families were reunited.

William waited anxiously as load after load of passengers came ashore. He hoped that his son John was aboard, as well as Pastor John Robinson. Perhaps even Alice Southworth might have heeded his letter and would be on the *Anne*. Sadly, William soon learned that neither his son nor John Robinson was among the passengers on the ship. As he tried to temper his disappointment, he spotted Alice being rowed ashore in the longboat. For a moment he felt bashful. If she was among the passengers and had risked such a dangerous journey, it was surely because she had come to be his wife. When the longboat came ashore, William stepped forward and welcomed Alice as he helped her from the boat. Sure enough, as the two of them walked through the gates that opened onto the beach and into Plymouth Town, Alice confirmed that she had indeed come to marry him.

William walked Alice up the main street of town to show her the governor's house where he now lived. The house was located in the center of town, where the street that led up from the beach to the fort on The Mount crossed another street that ran parallel to the beach. The clapboard house was bigger than most of the other houses, since it was where William held meetings with his advisors and conducted the business of running the colony.

The following morning William learned that a number of the new arrivals were shocked by the conditions of Plymouth. He supposed that many had imagined the place to be more like an English town, with sturdy, well-appointed houses and ample supplies on hand. Some of the people told him that they wished they'd never left England and said they planned to return home as soon as possible. William could not blame them. He knew it must be shocking for them to see the state of the community's residents, who were emaciated and weak. Most of them were dressed in clothes that were scarcely more than rags.

Ten days later the second ship arrived at Plymouth. It was the *Little James*, a small, two-masted vessel used mostly for coastal trade in England. The *Little James* had been sent by the Merchant Adventurers to stay in Plymouth for the colonists to use as a fishing vessel. William found this a little ironic, since the colonists had already proven to be terrible fishermen. The *Little James* carried another thirty passengers, along with some supplies.

On board the *Little James* was a letter for William from Robert Cushman, who was serving as the colony's representative in England. Robert seemed to have been able to stir those investors who remained a part of the Merchant Adventurers to take a greater interest in the well-being of the colony. In his letter, Robert apologized for not sending more supplies and for sending so many Strangers who were "none of the fittest" men. William had already come to that conclusion, nor was he happy about a group of ten men called Particulars who arrived on the *Anne*. These men, who had paid the Merchant Adventurers for their passage to Plymouth, were entitled to live in Plymouth but not required to do any work for the colony's benefit. They could do whatever they wanted as long as they each placed one bushel of Indian wheat into the common storehouse each year. William thought that having men in the community who were not required to pitch in their labor for the good of all would only lead to trouble and discontent among the other residents.

William had other things to worry about, however. With all of the newcomers, the population of Plymouth had almost doubled. The extra helping hands in the community were much needed, but they had to be accommodated and fed. New cottages would have to be built for them. And the piles of oak clapboards and animal pelts stored up in Plymouth needed to be loaded aboard the *Anne* for shipment back to England.

As he looked at all the new arrivals, William wished that more of them were Separatists from Leyden. After all, Plymouth was the place they had dreamed about and planned for years. Instead, most of the ninety-plus newcomers were Strangers. Nonetheless, Alice Southworth had been on the *Anne*, and William looked forward to his life with her.

Chapter 14

Conspiracy

On Thursday, August 14, 1623, William Bradford and Alice Southworth were married at the governor's house in Plymouth. As was normal for Separatists, it was a civil ceremony, conducted by Isaac Allerton, William's assistant. Alice wore a dark dress with a lace collar, and William had on a grey suit and his purple governor's robe. The whole community gathered for the event. Also in attendance was Massasoit, along with one of his five wives and 120 braves.

A great celebration was held after the wedding ceremony. Massasoit brought four deer and a turkey to help feed the crowd. The deer and turkey were roasted on spits over a fire, and pots of stew simmered beside the flames. Pastries were served, along with grapes and plums, plus a variety of berries gathered from the woods around Plymouth. Following the feast, the Indians entertained everyone with their boisterous dances.

As he watched the dancing while seated beside Alice, William felt contented. At thirty-three years of age, he was a married man again. He looked forward to Alice's companionship and being able to sit and talk in depth to someone other than his advisors. He had missed that intimate companionship after Dorothy died. Of course, it wouldn't just be William and Alice living in the governor's house. Also sharing the house were Thomas Cushman and several children whose parents had died during the first winter in Plymouth and whom William now cared for. William hoped that it wouldn't be too long before his household grew. Alice had left her two sons behind in Leyden with relatives, and William hoped that they, along with his own son, John, would be reunited under one roof in Plymouth.

A short while after the wedding, the *Anne* pulled up anchor and headed out to sea on its way back to England. William hoped that the cargo loaded in its hold would fetch a good price in London and allow the colonists to reduce their indebtedness to the Merchant Adventurers. Also traveling on the *Anne* were a number of the Particulars who had decided that life in New England was not for them. William was happy to see them go.

Edward Winslow was also onboard. William had dispatched him to London to update the Merchant Adventurers on the community's progress and to try to arrange extra and more regular supplies from them. Edward was also to ask them not to send over any more Strangers or Particulars but rather to send more Separatists from Leyden, particularly Pastor John Robinson. As far as William was concerned, the balance of Separatists to Strangers in Plymouth was off. Plymouth had always been intended as a Separatist community where they could practice their religion unhindered by Church of England edicts. But the Separatists were now a minority in the settlement they had set out to establish.

With the *Anne* on her way back to England, it was time for the community to turn its attention to the harvest. The corn stalks were laden with ears of corn, and the settlers eagerly set to work harvesting their household plots. The decision to allow them to have these plots had been a good one. It was a bountiful harvest of not only corn but also beans and squash growing between the rows. When everything was gathered in from the fields, it was their biggest harvest ever. William breathed a sigh of relief. It had seemed early on that the drought-parched crop was going to be a complete failure, but he knew that God had heard their prayers and blessed their harvest. William was both humbled and delighted. The harvest was big enough to put an immediate end to the constant hunger that the people had endured and to have plenty of corn left over to store for the winter ahead.

As the months rolled on, William went about the task of administering Plymouth. Enough cottages had been erected to house all the new arrivals. As winter approached with an adequate supply of food

on hand, William felt a sense of contentment. Plymouth seemed to be getting on its feet. Living there
was still a challenge, but William hoped that the
life-or-death struggle for daily survival was behind
them. He was also content in his marriage to Alice
and elated when he learned she was pregnant.

As spring approached in March 1624, it was
once again time to elect the colony's governor. William had held the position for three years and had
grown weary. With a new wife and a baby on the
way, he decided it was time for somebody else to
take on the role. The residents of Plymouth were not
so eager to replace William. They felt he had done an
admirable job and elected him to govern the colony
once more. With Plymouth continuing to grow, the
job of governor was also growing. William negotiated
with the community to allow him five assistants to
spread the workload around.

One of the first things William dealt with in his
new term as governor was a request submitted by
members of the community. Given how successful
the harvest had been the year before with individual
households working plots assigned to them, these
settlers asked for permanent ownership of their own
plots. They argued that residents would work the
land even harder if they owned and controlled it outright. William agreed with their reasoning. Having
their own plot to work had made the residents of
Plymouth more productive, and he hoped that own-
ing the land outright would make them even more
productive. Each person in Plymouth was assigned
an acre of land to own, as close to town as possible.

No sooner had William settled this matter in spring 1624 than another ship sailed into the harbor. It was the *Charity*, and onboard was Edward Winslow on his way back from London. Edward handed William a letter from Robert Cushman offering his apologies for not sending more luxury items such as butter and sugar. There had simply not been enough money to pay for such things. Nonetheless, the *Charity* carried much-needed supplies for the residents of Plymouth, along with items to be used in trading with the Indians. The Merchant Adventurers had loaded the ship with proper fishing gear to help the colonists support themselves as fishermen. To that end, the *Charity* also had a boatbuilder aboard, hired by the Merchant Adventurers to stay in Plymouth and build a fleet of fishing vessels. There was also a salt maker on the ship who would stay in Plymouth to provide the salt necessary to salt the fish they caught before shipping them back to England.

William appreciated the sentiment involved, but the truth was that the colonists were terrible fishermen and more boats and better gear were probably not going to change that. But the *Charity* carried something William had specifically requested that Edward return with—three heifers and a bull. William hoped that these animals would form the basis of the first herd of cattle in New England.

The *Charity* also carried someone whose presence on the ship William found hard to fathom: the Reverend John Lyford. William had been expecting Pastor John Robinson, but the Merchant Adventurers had instead sent a Church of England clergyman, a man who represented the very religious institution from which William and his fellow Separatists had separated themselves. Edward explained that the remaining Merchant Adventurers were mostly staunch members of the Church of England and were not inclined to send over any more Separatists from Leyden. They had chosen an Anglican minister and his family to look after the spiritual needs of Anglicans who numbered more than Separatists in Plymouth.

William felt betrayed by Plymouth's financial backers. When the Separatists had received their original land patent for Virginia, it had taken so long to get because they insisted upon a clause granting them religious freedom. Now here they were, anything but religiously free. Instead, Separatists in Leyden who longed to join them in Plymouth were purposefully not being transported over, while the Plymouth Separatists were saddled with a Church of England minister and expected to feed and house him and his wife and five children.

William's attitude toward John Lyford softened as he got to know him. John seemed humble and accepting of the Separatists and their beliefs. In fact, much to William's surprise, John asked to become a member of the Plymouth church the Separatists had established. Before long he was invited to join William Brewster, William, and his five governing assistants as a member of what was now called the Governor's Council.

In the spring William had to deal with another man—John Oldham, a Particular who had come over on the *Anne* the year before and was one of the few who did not return to England. William wished that he had left, because the man was a constant irritant in the community. John came to William to beg forgiveness, saying that he had done the Separatists harm by complaining about them to others in the community and by writing letters to England saying slanderous things about them. He apologized for his behavior and confessed that he'd had a change of heart and wanted to mend his ways. William graciously accepted John's apology and allowed him to stay on in the community.

Meanwhile, the boatbuilder the Merchant Adventurers had sent over proved to be a skilled craftsman and was soon hard at work building several new shallops to be used for fishing. The salt maker, though, seemed to be far less skilled at his craft and failed to produce any salt, though he talked as if he were producing tons of it.

Since Alice was pregnant, William did as much as he could to take some of the load of managing the household off her shoulders.

The governor's house, located right in the center of Plymouth, provided William with a good place to see what was going on in the community. As he worked away in the house on administrative duties, William began to notice John Oldham and John Lyford spending time together. At first he thought nothing of it, but his suspicions were raised when John Billington and several others from the community began to join them. The Billington family had been troublemakers in the community from the moment the *Mayflower* set sail from Plymouth, England.

William also noticed that when he was not with the others, John Lyford spent most of his time writing long letters. William began to suspect that some kind of conspiracy was being hatched, perhaps one to overthrow him and the Separatists and place Plymouth firmly under the control of the Church of England.

Now that he suspected a conspiracy, William quietly looked for an opportunity to confront it. The *Charity* had not yet left New England for England but had sailed north on a fishing expedition. When the vessel called at Plymouth again on its way back to England, William observed John Lyford and John Oldham hand over a large bundle of letters to the captain. After seeing this, William talked to William Brewster and several of his most trusted Separatist advisors to decide what to do.

Soon after the *Charity* raised anchor and sailed away from Plymouth, William and the others climbed into the shallop and set sail as though they were crossing the bay. However, they were following the *Charity*, and when the vessel was well out of sight of Plymouth, they intercepted the ship and went aboard.

On the ship William found almost two dozen letters written by John Lyford and John Oldham. As he read them, he was astounded. The letters were filled with lies and slander. They advised the Merchant Adventurers to send over as many Strangers as possible to overwhelm the Separatists and to never let another person from Leyden, most notably their pastor, John Robinson, come to Plymouth. According to the letters, it was time to get rid of the current leadership of the community and bring Plymouth firmly under the control of the Church of England. William's suspicions had been right. Together with his advisors, William spent several hours copying some of the letters and confiscated others.

With their work on the *Charity* done, the group headed back to Plymouth in the shallop. Back in Plymouth William and his advisors told no one about the conspiracy or what they had found. Instead, they waited for the right opportunity to act. William did not have to wait long. Soon afterward John Oldham refused to show up for guard duty when ordered to do so by Myles Standish. Instead he got into an argument with Myles and pulled a knife on him. Oldham was arrested and locked up in the fort. Now William waited for John Lyford to slip up, which he did when he openly held a Church of England service in violation of the colony's rules. He too was arrested.

William called the community together at the fort for a court to hear the charges against the two men. Once the court was assembled, William told John Oldham and John Lyford that they were charged with "plotting against them and disturbing the peace, both in respecte of their civill & church state." Both men said that there was absolutely no proof that either of them had committed such crimes. William watched their faces drop as he pulled out the letters intercepted from the *Charity* and began to read them aloud. A hush fell over the room. John Lyford hung his head and stood motionless.

The two men were quickly found guilty. As he passed judgment on them, William explained that what they had done amounted to treason. Both were to be banished from Plymouth, John Oldham immediately. John Lyford, who showed contrition before the court and begged for forgiveness, was given six months to organize his affairs before banishment.

William felt that justice had been served and the conspiracy crushed. Now he had other things to concern himself with. On Thursday, June 17, 1624, Alice Bradford, attended by Bridget Fuller, Plymouth's midwife, gave birth to a son, whom they named William Bradford Jr. William was delighted. As he held his new son in his arms, he couldn't help but think about the birth of his first son John in Leyden nine years before. How he wished John was there to see his new brother.

New life was springing forth in other places besides the Bradford home. While William had been busy unraveling the conspiracy, the colonists had planted their corn on their lots. The shoots were now out of the ground, lush and green and growing rapidly. Already it was time to plant the beans and squash between the rows. It seemed to William that Plymouth was flourishing. He had hopes of an even more bountiful harvest than the year before, and once again they had a decent supply of trade goods on hand to trade for beaver and otter pelts. Best of all for William, the constant starvation the colonists had endured during the first two years of the settlement seemed well behind them.

Throughout the summer the residents tended their crops, and William Jr. grew quickly. William's only disappointment during the summer was the death of the boatbuilder, who had completed two new boats. Two more lay unfinished at the time of his death. As for the salt maker, he had completely given up on his endeavor but chose to stay on in Plymouth.

In the fall the residents gathered in their largest harvest of corn, beans, and squash. They had more than enough corn and beans to feed the community throughout the winter. As usual, winter descended with its icy coldness over New England. It was easier to endure with adequate food on hand, and the constant improvements to housing meant that the cottages were much snugger and warmer than they had ever been.

The year 1625 rolled around, and William delighted in watching his young son's first attempts at crawling. All seemed well in Plymouth until a passing ship delivered a letter to William. All was not well in London. Although John Lyford had begged for forgiveness at his trial, he had not given up his conspiratorial ways. Somehow he managed to have several letters describing his treatment by William and the leaders of Plymouth smuggled out of the community to London, where they had caused an uproar among the Merchant Adventurers. Many of the investors were incensed by the treatment meted out to a clergyman of the Church of England. It seemed as though the remaining group of Merchant Adventurers might split, leaving Plymouth facing an uncertain future.

William decided that something needed to be done to save their relationship with the Merchant

Adventurers in the short term. In the long term, he knew that the colonists needed to find a better solution than always being at the whim of their investors. In the spring William sent Myles Standish in the *Little James* to London. Before Myles set sail, the ship was loaded with salted cod and beaver pelts, enough, William reckoned, to pay off a quarter of the debt they owed their investors. William also charged Myles with approaching the Council for New England to see if there was any way Plymouth might be freed from its ties to the Merchant Adventurers.

Almost a year passed before Myles returned from England in early 1626. Although William hoped that he would bring good news, most of it was not. The Council for New England had offered no help, and Myles had approached the Merchant Adventurers about the situation. At first the investors were somewhat angry, especially since the *Little James* and all its cargo had been stolen by privateers shortly before the vessel reached England—another financial loss. Nonetheless, Myles had managed to get the investors to agree to negotiate with the colonists to buy them out and take full control of Plymouth. William saw some hope in this, and in the news that King James I of England had died and his son, Charles I, was now king. William hoped that the new king wouldn't follow the practices of his father in relation to the church and would instead let Englishmen practice religion according to their conscience.

Myles also relayed some news that was a bitter blow to William. Pastor John Robinson was dead, as was Robert Cushman. At the time of Myles's visit,

London was being ravaged by the plague, from which Robert had died. William hung his head at the news, his heart heavy with loss. But he was the governor of Plymouth, and despite the bad news, the people of the community looked to him for leadership.

Undertakers

Meanwhile, the routine of daily living went on in Plymouth. In March William was reelected governor for a fifth term. Not long afterward he conducted the marriage ceremony of Isaac Allerton, his assistant governor, to Fear Brewster, daughter of William and Mary Brewster.

In late spring, crops were planted and the settlement's residents kept busy tending the fields. By now the residents of Plymouth were raising chickens, goats, and pigs on their plots of land. The cattle that Edward had brought from England were breeding. William hoped that more cows would arrive from England and help speed the process of creating a herd.

The trading of pelts with the Indians also carried on. In this regard, William kept an eye on the Dutch, who had founded a colony known as New Amsterdam on an island at the mouth of the Hudson River, the same location the New Netherlands Company had wanted the Separatists to settle. From there the Dutch had also begun trading with the Indians along the southern New England coast and were potential competition to Plymouth's trading efforts.

As the year rolled on, William dispatched Isaac to London to negotiate with the Merchant Adventurers. In early 1627 Isaac returned with an agreement in which the Merchant Adventurers agreed to sell the colony outright for eighteen hundred pounds, to be paid in nine installments of two hundred pounds each year. William was delighted. The colonists at Plymouth would no longer be dependent upon a group of investors who, as far as he could see, didn't always have the best interests of the colony at heart. Of course, this raised the issue of ownership: If the colonists owned their colony, how should the assets be divided? It was decided that each single man or head of a family in the community would become a "purchaser," and purchasers would be given twenty acres of land and a house.

William felt this was a fair arrangement. Yet the money to buy the colony had to be raised and payments made in a timely manner. To this end, the "Undertakers" were established. This was a group of eight men, including William, William Brewster, Isaac Allerton, Edward Winslow, Myles Standish, John Alden, Thomas Prence, and John Howland. Together they would undertake both the payment of the eighteen hundred pounds owed to the Merchant

Adventurers and the payment of an additional six hundred pounds owed to other investors. To raise the money, the Undertakers would import from England various necessities to the colony. They would trade the imported items to the settlers for a fixed amount of corn, which would eventually be sold for profit. Because of the financial risk the Undertakers would carry, they were granted a six-year monopoly on trade with the Indians. Any profit the group made after paying Plymouth's debts would be theirs to keep.

Although William was not an experienced businessman or good at managing money, he trusted the input of the other Undertakers that it was a good arrangement and happily left Isaac in charge of taking care of the details. He was relieved that a plan was in place to be rid of the Merchant Adventurers.

In May 1627, soon after the Undertakers had been established, William became a father again when Alice gave birth to a daughter, whom they named Mercy. By now William Jr. was almost three years old. Other changes in the Bradford household had also taken place. Now that Robert Cushman was dead, William formally adopted Robert's nineteen-year-old son Thomas. In addition, twelve-year-old John Bradford finally arrived from Leyden to live with his father and stepmother. He arrived on a ship carrying thirty-five others from Leyden. For William, being reunited with his oldest son proved bittersweet. Although he had tried hard, the eight years the two had spent apart were not easily bridged. William's relationship with John was not close, and

John seemed to have a hard time adjusting to the busy Bradford household.

With the new arrangement to buy the colony in place and Plymouth's food supply now stable, William decided it was time for the colony to become more focused on trading with the Indians. Beaver pelts, in particular, which were in demand in England for making coats and hats, fetched a high price at market. As a result, a trading post was set up at Aptucxet, located at the head of Buzzards Bay to the south. There they traded blankets, bowls, metal tools, and other items for pelts. Soon afterward a trading post was established to the north on the Kennebec River.

During 1627, William received a letter from Peter Minuit, governor of the Dutch settlement of New Amsterdam, inviting the colonists at Plymouth to trade with New Amsterdam. William wrote a letter of reply in Dutch, saying that Plymouth was well stocked with everything it needed for the year ahead. Undeterred, Isaak de Rasieres, the chief trader at New Amsterdam, showed up in Plymouth in October 1627. He came with sugar, linen, and other cloth made in Holland. William liked Isaak, and the fact that William could converse with him in fluent Dutch seemed to impress his guest. The two talked about trading with the Indians. One thing Isaak talked about fascinated William: wampum. Isaak explained that wampum was a form of currency that came in two types, black and white. White wampum was made from periwinkle shells, and black wampum, from clam shells. White wampum was more valuable than the black. The shells were fashioned into small cylinders and polished, and Indians strung them on strings to form money belts. William had never heard of such a thing and was skeptical. Nonetheless, Isaak convinced him to buy fifty pounds' worth of wampum and find out for himself if it worked.

At first William thought Isaak had defrauded him. The Indians around Plymouth were not interested in trading pelts for wampum. But the inland tribes were more than happy to trade for it. Seeing the brisk trade that developed with these tribes, some of the coastal Indians also began to accept trading pelts for wampum.

William was happy. Trading pelts for wampum was much more economical than trading goods that needed to be imported from England. As Plymouth's trading enterprise flourished, the Undertakers were delighted. With beaver and otter pelts rolling into the colony's trading posts, they could see that they would be able to make their scheduled payments to the Merchant Adventurers. In mid-1628 Isaac Allerton set out for England on a ship loaded with enough pelts to pay off three hundred pounds of their debt.

While things were going well in Plymouth, a situation developed farther up the coast that required William's attention. Two years before, a settlement called Mount Wollaston had been established just north of Wessagusset. The settlement consisted of about thirty-five men led by Captain Wollaston and his business partner, Thomas Morton. The year before, Captain Wollaston had moved to Virginia, leaving the settlement in Thomas's hands.

After the experience with the colony at Wessagusset, William was always wary of new settlements.
His doubts were realized after word filtered back to
Plymouth that Thomas had renamed the place Mare
Mount and had erected a maypole around which the
residents drank, sang, danced, and partied with the
crews of passing ships and with Indian braves and
Indian women. Such behavior was considered scan-
dalous in Plymouth, particularly by the Separatists,
who took to calling the settlement Merrymount. William took to referring to Thomas Morton as Lord of
Misrule.

Those at Plymouth learned to ignore the behavior taking place at Merrymount, until Thomas began
trading liquor, muskets, gunpowder, and shot to
the Indians. William believed that putting such
items into the hands of the Indians endangered all
Englishmen in New England. He was not the only
one who felt this way. By now several small English settlements were scattered along the coast of
New England. The leaders of these settlements wrote
to William asking for help in putting an end to the
practices taking place at Merrymount.

William sent a warning letter to Thomas Morton
to stop his dangerous trading practices. But when
Thomas sent back a rude reply, William decided
to act decisively. He dispatched Myles Standish,
accompanied by nine armed men, to deal with the
situation at Merrymount.

Once again William waited at Plymouth for news.
It didn't take Myles long to return with good news.
He reported that when they arrived at Merrymount,

they found Thomas Morton and his men locked in their house with a small arsenal of weapons at the ready. When asked to surrender, the men jeered and laughed at Myles and then rushed out the door to attack him and his men. But the Merrymount men were so drunk that they couldn't aim their muskets. Thomas, holding his gun, rushed at Myles, who knocked the musket aside and captured him. The whole fight was over almost before it started. Myles brought Thomas back to Plymouth, where he was kept under arrest until he was bundled onto a ship and exiled back to England. Meanwhile the remaining men at Merrymount quickly disbanded. For William, it was a good outcome. Thomas Morton was on his way back to England, and William was glad to be rid of him and Merrymount.

Shortly afterward, Alice's two sons, Thomas and Constant Southworth, arrived in Plymouth. William welcomed his two new stepsons into the Bradford household.

In September 1628, William learned that fifty Puritan settlers had landed at the Naumkeag colony, founded two years before to the north of Massachusetts Bay. The group was led by John Endecott, who changed the colony's name to Salem. John was one of six Puritans who had secured a land patent for what was being called Massachusetts Bay Colony.

William was not surprised that Puritans were beginning to flee England. Following the death of his father, King Charles I began to clamp down even harder on English nonconformists. In particular, Puritans were being thrown into jail, fined, stripped of their property, and sometimes executed for their beliefs. Under this constant harassment, many Puritans began looking longingly at America. They dreamed of a colony there much like the one the Separatists had built at Plymouth where they could be free from the religious tyranny of the king.

As the first small groups of Puritans arrived in New England, William realized it was not going to be easy for them. They would endure many struggles along the way. Indeed, the winter of 1628–29 was the coldest William could remember since arriving in the New World. Just as starvation and sickness had been constant threats to Plymouth nine years before, so too were they in Salem. Half the new arrivals died from the cold, lack of food, and disease. William sent Samuel Fuller, Plymouth's surgeon, to Salem to help the survivors.

With the arrival of spring in 1629, life at Plymouth once again fell into a routine of trading with the Indians at the trading posts along the coast and preparing the ground for new crops. By now more cattle had arrived from England, and the process of breeding a good herd continued. Already the cows were producing milk to make butter, a much-enjoyed commodity in Plymouth.

William's reelection in March 1630 marked his ninth year as governor of Plymouth. The year was to be a challenging one for him. It had some high points: Alice gave birth to another son, whom they named Joseph. Isaac Allerton returned from England with a land patent for their trading post located at Cushnoc on the Kennebec River. The final shipload of Separatists arrived from Leyden, ten years after the first group had arrived. William wasn't much impressed, however, with this group of new arrivals.

The first challenge William faced was Isaac Allerton, who had been taking care of Plymouth's business affairs in London for the previous three years. Isaac had made several trips across the Atlantic on ships loaded with pelts worth thousands of pounds. Some of the money for the pelts was to be used to pay off the Undertakers' debt to the Merchant Adventurers directly, and some of it was to be used to buy trade goods and other commodities for the colony. Isaac also represented the colony in negotiations with various English officials. The Undertakers trusted him to take care of the colony's affairs for their good and the good of everyone else at Plymouth. William was flabbergasted, however, when Isaac arrived back in Plymouth from London with Thomas Morton and announced that he'd hired the man to be his assistant. It was inconceivable to William that a Separatist could make such a decision. Not only had Lord of Misrule, as William referred to Thomas, been exiled from New England, but also his character was clearly so ungodly and profane that it made William question Isaac's own character.

William would not allow Thomas to stay in Plymouth, and Thomas was soon banished from the settlement. With him gone, William and the other Undertakers decided to investigate how Isaac was conducting their business. Having shown such bad judgment concerning Thomas Morton, might he have exercised bad judgment in handling their business?

The Untertakers soon discovered that Isaac exhibited a pattern of mixing his own business affairs with those of the colony. Isaac would buy trade goods for the colony and then set aside the best goods for his own trading ventures back in Plymouth. He often charged the Undertakers twice for some of the merchandise he purchased and shipped back, pocketing the extra money. He would also charge them exaggerated fees for his expenses while in England, again pocketing the extra money. In this way he had managed to steal hundreds of pounds from the Undertakers. William was devastated: his trusted assistant and fellow Separatist was a cheat and a thief.

As the Undertakers began unraveling Isaac's complicated business dealings, they discovered that they still owed one thousand pounds to the Merchant Adventurers, far more than they believed they owed by now. To William's disbelief, the six hundred pounds owed to other investors in 1627 had risen to nearly five thousand pounds, which William and the remaining Undertakers were responsible for repaying.

Isaac was immediately removed from his position, not only as the colony's business manager, but also as William's assistant and advisor. William found himself in a difficult position. Were Isaac any other man, he would have banished him from the colony, but Isaac had been with the Separatists from the beginning, first in Leyden and then in the New World. He had signed the Mayflower Compact and worked hard to help establish Plymouth. He was also married to William Brewster's daughter. To William these were things not easily overlooked. While he knew it would now take years for the Undertakers to repay their debts, William chose to forgive Isaac and allowed him to stay in Plymouth. While he found it hard to understand Isaac's betrayal of his covenant with God, his church, and his fellow colonists, William felt that it was for God to judge, while it was his job to offer mercy and forgiveness.

The second challenge for William also involved a signer of the Mayflower Compact. John Billington had gotten into a heated argument with his neighbor, John Newcomen, and had shot him dead. Billington was arrested and put on trial in Plymouth, where he was found guilty of murder and sentenced to death. William found the responsibility of ordering the execution of a person who had sailed on the Mayflower with him and had signed the Mayflower Compact difficult to bear.

Over the summer of 1630, a fleet of eleven ships carrying nearly a thousand Puritans had arrived in Massachusetts Bay. Some of the new arrivals settled in Salem, while others established another settlement beside the bay on the banks of the Charles River, which they named Boston. John Winthrop was the leader of the fleet of ships, and he was now the official governor of Massachusetts Bay Colony. William decided to write to John Winthrop and seek his advice in the matter of the execution of John Billington. He'd heard that John was a lawyer.

John soon replied to William's letter, informing him that he concurred with the court's decision and sentence and that John Billington ought to be executed as soon as possible for his crime. Although it was in William's nature to forgive, in September 1630 he gave the order for John to be hanged. The execution, the first of an Englishman carried out in New England, was administered by Myles Standish.

As 1630 drew to a close, William reflected on his life. Ten years had passed since he and the other Separatists and the Strangers had set out from England on the *Mayflower* for the New World. Since their arrival, much had been achieved. In fact, William had just begun writing a history of Plymouth, chronicling each year of the settlement's existence. As he wrote, he could see that they still had much more to do. From Plymouth, William also kept a wary eye on the growing number of Puritan colonists arriving at Massachusetts Bay.

Chapter 16

Breaking Apart

Not long after John Billington's execution, William traveled north to Boston to meet John Winthrop in person. He liked the new governor of Massachusetts Bay Colony. He felt that John was a gentleman, a Christian with whom he could deal honorably. In Boston William got to see just how organized and well-financed this influx of Puritans was. The group arrived with ample supplies to take care of their needs, and a steady flow of ships between Massachusetts Bay and England was ferrying more Puritan settlers and supplies across the Atlantic. It felt odd to William to be standing in a settlement whose population in just a few months had grown to three times that of Plymouth.

William felt a surge of pride during his visit when Governor Winthrop asked him details about how the

Separatist church in Plymouth operated. William explained how church leaders in Plymouth were not appointed to their positions but were elected by the members of the congregation. John seemed to like this approach and told William he intended to model the Puritan churches in New England on it.

After arriving back in Plymouth, William again was wary. The sheer size and wealth of the colony at Massachusetts Bay could pose a threat to Plymouth. With more and more Puritans arriving from England, William was sure that it wouldn't be long before they began casting their eyes on land under the control of Plymouth and wanting some of it for themselves. And there would be competition for trade with the Indians, something the Plymouth colonists had worked hard to develop and relied upon.

Having such a large colony located nearby also had a good side. The Puritans were generally wealthy, and they provided a market for the corn, beans, and other crops the colonists at Plymouth grew and for the cattle, goats, pigs, and chickens they raised. As a result, the price for these commodities began to increase rapidly. The demand for them was so great that Plymouth couldn't keep up with it.

This situation created another challenge for the residents of Plymouth, who now needed more land to farm. William responded by giving them bigger allotments of land, but these allotments were located farther and farther away from town. Whereas the colonists used to walk to their land and farm it during the day, returning to Plymouth at night, now they started building houses on their far-flung landholdings. For William this was hard to watch. His vision, and that of the Separatists from the start back in Leyden, had always been for a strong, tight-knit central community based upon Christian principles and centered around church. But with people moving out of Plymouth, hopes of that dream ever being realized began to fade.

William was disappointed about another thing that lessened the importance of Plymouth. Since its founding, the settlement had been where trading ships docked when they arrived in New England. It was the largest and most important stopping point along the coast. But now those ships bypassed Plymouth and went straight to Boston, with its deep harbor and wealthy citizens.

More unwelcome changes occurred. A year after the Puritans settled in Boston, Myles Standish, John Alden, and William Brewster's oldest son, Jonathan, all had moved out of Plymouth to the north shore of Plymouth Bay, where they founded the town of Duxbury. In 1632 the residents of Duxbury received permission from the Plymouth church to start their own congregation in their community. This was another blow for William. The Plymouth church was supposed to be the linchpin of the community, the place where all residents came together united before God. Now that too was breaking apart. Three of his close companions and their families had chosen to move ten miles away.

Soon after the founding of Duxbury, a group of residents from Plymouth established the town of Scituate, farther north of Duxbury on the coast. Then

Marshfield, situated between Scituate and Duxbury, was founded. To the south of Plymouth, residents left town to establish Sandwich, and then Barnstable and Yarmouth on Cape Cod. As these towns were founded, they began to attract settlers, some from England but many from Massachusetts Bay Colony.

William found it hard not to view each new town as a betrayal of the Separatists' original goal. He was also dismayed that while the population of Boston grew rapidly, Plymouth's population declined. "And no man now thought he could live, except he had catle and a great deale of ground to keep them; all striving to increase their flocks. By which means they were scatered all over the Bay quickly and the towne, in which they lived compactly until now, was left very thine and in a short time allmost desolate," he wrote in his history of the colony.

In 1633 Isaac Allerton's wife, Fear, died, and shortly afterward Isaac left Plymouth and moved to New Amsterdam. Also during 1633 William decided it was time to take a break from being governor, which he had been for twelve years. Edward Winslow was elected to the position. William enjoyed the change. He was able to spend more time tending to his landholdings and taking time with his children, since he was also their schoolteacher. The children were growing fast. John was now eighteen years old, William Jr. nine, Mercy six, and Joseph three. William himself was forty-three years old.

Thomas Prence became governor in 1634, and in 1635 William was again elected. The year before, during Thomas Prence's governorship, had been a bad year for Plymouth's trading efforts with the Indians. Traders from Massachusetts Bay Colony had ousted the Plymouth traders from their trading post on the Kennebec River. At their trading post at Matianuck on the Connecticut River, a group of Puritan settlers arrived and took over the place for their settlement. Constant struggles over boundaries ensued as the Puritans kept encroaching on land belonging to Plymouth. William was often at loggerheads with John Winthrop over these issues, which were invariably settled by Plymouth losing a little more of its territory. The outcome infuriated William, but he was not prepared to use force against the Puritans with whom he shared a common faith.

Plymouth had always been governed in an informal way, with the governor and his council responding to situations as they arose and creating written laws where necessary. But by 1636, with six new settlements spread throughout the colony, this approach no longer worked. It was time for a more formalized approach to governing.

With his assistants and representatives from the settlements, William drew up what was called the General Fundamentals, which laid out the basic governing principles of Plymouth Colony. The document stated that laws could not be made nor taxes levied without all the freemen of the community consenting in a legally assembled body. An annual election of the governor and his assistants was to be held. Criminal offenders were guaranteed trial by a jury consisting of twelve men, and the offender could challenge any of his jurors. Also, no person could be condemned or sentenced at trial without the testimony of at least two individuals or without sufficient circumstantial evidence. All freemen who had moved away to outlying settlements were required to travel to Plymouth Town three times a year to attend the general court, where various matters relating to the colony could be discussed and voted on.

During the following year, 1637, the Puritan settlers who had taken over Plymouth's trading post at Matianuck on the Connecticut River began being attacked by the Pequot Indians who lived in the area. A number of settlers were killed as they tended their fields or hunted for food in the forest. The Pequots were also trying to turn the Narragansetts against the English. Something had to be done. Governor John Winthrop asked William to provide a contingent of armed men to join armed Puritans to deal with the problem. William agreed, and the force marched off to Connecticut.

William was not pleased when he later learned that it turned out to be a bloody, one-sided encounter in which almost all the Pequot—men, women, and children—were killed. Those who survived were rounded up and sold as slaves. William disliked violence, and yet he felt the Pequots had made clear their intentions to kill New England settlers.

With the threat of the Pequots removed, William turned his focus back onto Plymouth. The freemen living in the outlying settlements had grown tired of traveling to Plymouth Town three times a year for general court meetings. William instituted a new representative approach to governing Plymouth Colony. Those living in the outlying settlements would elect two men as their representatives at general court meetings, while Plymouth Town would elect four representatives. This freed everyone but the representatives from regularly traveling to Plymouth Town.

As 1640 rolled around, William fretted that Plymouth was less of a unified Christian community than it had been a decade before. Nearly three thousand people were now living in the colony, but they were spread across a number of towns. A large portion of the colony's population rarely came to Plymouth Town, whose population had now dropped to about 150, the same number that lived there in 1623.

William liked to sit and talk with William Brewster, who had been like a father to him as a young man. Now, as the chief elder in the Plymouth church, William Brewster was William's spiritual and temporal advisor and close friend. The two reminisced about their lives in Yorkshire and the Scrooby Separatist group, their flight to Holland, and the move to the New World. But always as they talked, their voices were tinged with the regret of not being able to create in America the community they had dreamed of.

Although disappointed by the direction Plymouth had taken, William continued to serve the colony faithfully. He kept writing his history of the colony and tried to be a steadying influence in the lives of those around him. From time to time Massasoit would come to Plymouth to visit, and the two men would talk together. Despite all the upheaval going on in the countryside around them, Massasoit and those at Plymouth Colony remained true to the peace treaty they had made with each other.

On Tuesday, April 18, 1643, at the age of eighty, William Brewster died. It was a blow to William, a "matter of great sadness and mourning" he wrote. Of his friend he noted, "For his personal abilities, he was qualified above many." Somehow Plymouth seemed lonely without his old friend around to talk to and to rely upon for support and counsel.

In 1644 William could barely believe it when a group of Plymouth residents proposed abandoning the present town and moving across Cape Cod Bay. They argued that it was a more hospitable site, where a new town could be established that they hoped would attract a bigger population. William wondered how they could think of abandoning Plymouth. To him, Plymouth was the heart and soul of the colony. To move would be to give up on everything the Separatists had dreamed of when they had landed in New England. Thankfully, the plan to move Plymouth was abandoned, though several families, including Thomas Prence's, moved across the bay onto Cape Cod and established Eastham. Nonetheless, William continued as governor, though by now he did so from a sense of duty rather than idealism of what could be. When he was not conducting civic business, he loved to tend his land and herd of cattle.

In 1646 William suffered the loss of another close friend and associate, but this time not to death. Edward Winslow, who had been Plymouth's ambassador to the Indians and other settlements, decided to return to England. As Edward sailed away, his departure felt to William almost as if it were Edward's death. He supposed he would never see his old friend again.

During 1646 William added only a few lines to his history of Plymouth about the events that year. In 1647 he stopped recording events for each year and instead just wrote the year's date at the top of a blank page. He had nothing positive to report.

For the first time since his sickness at the founding of Plymouth, in 1648, at age fifty-eight, William complained about his health, writing that he had "bodily infirmities." And for the first time as governor his health prevented him from fulfilling some of his duties. Despite this, he pressed on. In the midst of his ill health, William's twenty-one-year-old daughter, Mercy, married Benjamin Vermayes.

At the age of sixty, in 1650, William began studying Hebrew. He wrote that he wanted to study "that most ancient language, and holy tongue, in which the Law and oracles of God were writ; and in which God, and angels, spake." And although he had given up on writing his history of Plymouth, he began writing poetry and essays on spiritual topics.

During that year his son John married Martha Bourne. And on Tuesday, April 23, of the same year William Jr., now twenty-five years old, married Alice Richards in Plymouth. As a wedding present, William deeded him some land.

William continued to suffer bouts of illness. In May 1653 he was too sick to attend the meeting of the general court, even though it was held in his house. William was aware that his body was growing weak, yet he pushed himself on, discharging his governor's duties as best he could.

On Friday, October 3, 1656, William mourned the death of yet another old friend from his days in

Leyden when Myles Standish died at age seventy-two. William knew he would miss the short, red-headed man with the fiery temper.

At the end of March 1657, William once again missed the meeting of the general court because of illness. It was also a difficult time for him and Alice as their daughter, Mercy, had just died at age twenty-nine.

William's body continued to weaken until on Thursday, May 7, 1657, he took to his bed and the next day wrote a will. At nine o'clock that evening, William Bradford died. He was sixty-seven years old.

Following his death, a volley of musket shots rang out as William's body was lowered into a grave on Fort Hill, which the settlers had once called The Mount. The residents of Plymouth mourned his death. For thirty-six years, William Bradford had led them unfailingly. He had been their rock.

Bibliography

Bradford, William. *Of Plymouth Plantation: The Pilgrims in America.* New York: Capricorn Books, 1962.

Bunker, Nick. *Making Haste from Babylon: The Mayflower Pilgrims and Their World.* New York: Alfred A. Knopf, 2010.

Demos, John. *A Little Commonwealth: Family Life in Plymouth Colony.* New York: Oxford University Press, 1970.

Doherty, Kieran. *William Bradford: Rock of Plymouth.* Brookfield, CT: Twenty-First Century Books, 1999.

Gragg, Rod. *The Pilgrim Chronicles: An Eyewitness History of the Pilgrims and the Founding of Plymouth Colony.* Washington, DC: Regnery History, 2014.

James, Sydney V., Jr., ed. *Three Visitors to Early Plymouth: Letters about the Pilgrim Settlement in New England During Its First Seven Years.* Plymouth, MA: Plimoth Plantation, 1963.

Johnson, Caleb. *Here Shall I Die Ashore: Stephen Hopkins; Bermuda Castaway, Jamestown Survivor, Mayflower Pilgrim.* N.p.: Xlibris, 2007.

Philbrick, Nathaniel. *Mayflower: A Story of Courage, Community, and War.* New York: Viking, 2006.

Schmidt, Gary D. *William Bradford: Plymouth's Faithful Pilgrim.* Grand Rapids: Eerdmans Books for Young Readers, 1999.

About the Authors

Janet and Geoff Benge are a husband and wife writing team with more than thirty years of writing experience. Janet is a former elementary school teacher. Geoff holds a degree in history. Together they have a passion to make history come alive for a new generation of readers.

Originally from New Zealand, the Benges make their home in the Orlando, Florida, area.

HEROES OF HISTORY are available in paperback, e-book, and audiobook formats, with more coming soon! Unit Study Curriculum Guides are available for each biography.

www.HeroesThenAndNow.com

Also from Janet and Geoff Benge...

More adventure-filled biographies for ages 10 to 100!

Heroes of History

Christian Heroes: Then & Now

Hudson Taylor: Deep in the Heart of China • *978-1-57658-016-5*
Amy Carmichael: Rescuer of Precious Gems • *978-1-57658-018-9*
Eric Liddell: Something Greater Than Gold • *978-1-57658-137-7*
Corrie ten Boom: Keeper of the Angels' Den • *978-1-57658-136-0*
William Carey: Obliged to Go • *978-1-57658-147-6*
George Müller: Guardian of Bristol's Orphans • *978-1-57658-145-2*
Jim Elliot: One Great Purpose • *978-1-57658-146-9*
Mary Slessor: Forward into Calabar • *978-1-57658-148-3*
David Livingstone: Africa's Trailblazer • *978-1-57658-153-7*
Betty Greene: Wings to Serve • *978-1-57658-152-0*
Adoniram Judson: Bound for Burma • *978-1-57658-161-2*
Cameron Townsend: Good News in Every Language • *978-1-57658-164-3*
Jonathan Goforth: An Open Door in China • *978-1-57658-174-2*
Lottie Moon: Giving Her All for China • *978-1-57658-188-9*
John Williams: Messenger of Peace • *978-1-57658-256-5*
William Booth: Soup, Soap, and Salvation • *978-1-57658-258-9*
Rowland Bingham: Into Africa's Interior • *978-1-57658-282-4*
Ida Scudder: Healing Bodies, Touching Hearts • *978-1-57658-285-5*
Wilfred Grenfell: Fisher of Men • *978-1-57658-292-3*
Lillian Trasher: The Greatest Wonder in Egypt • *978-1-57658-305-0*
Loren Cunningham: Into All the World • *978-1-57658-199-5*
Florence Young: Mission Accomplished • *978-1-57658-313-5*
Sundar Singh: Footprints Over the Mountains • *978-1-57658-318-0*
C. T. Studd: No Retreat • *978-1-57658-288-6*
Rachel Saint: A Star in the Jungle • *978-1-57658-337-1*
Brother Andrew: God's Secret Agent • *978-1-57658-355-5*
Clarence Jones: Mr. Radio • *978-1-57658-343-2*
Count Zinzendorf: Firstfruit • *978-1-57658-262-6*
John Wesley: The World His Parish • *978-1-57658-382-1*
C. S. Lewis: Master Storyteller • *978-1-57658-385-2*
David Bussau: Facing the World Head-on • *978-1-57658-415-6*
Jacob DeShazer: Forgive Your Enemies • *978-1-57658-475-0*
Isobel Kuhn: On the Roof of the World • *978-1-57658-497-2*
Elisabeth Elliot: Joyful Surrender • *978-1-57658-513-9*
Paul Brand: Helping Hands • *978-1-57658-536-8*
D. L. Moody: Bringing Souls to Christ • *978-1-57658-552-8*
Dietrich Bonhoeffer: In the Midst of Wickedness • *978-1-57658-713-3*

Francis Asbury: Circuit Rider • *978-1-57658-737-9*
Samuel Zwemer: The Burden of Arabia • *978-1-57658-738-6*
Klaus-Dieter John: Hope in the Land of the Incas • *978-1-57658-826-2*
Mildred Cable: Through the Jade Gate • *978-157658-886-4*
John Flynn: Into the Never Never • *978-1-57658-898-7*

Available in paperback, e-book, and audiobook formats.
Unit Study Curriculum Guides are available for many biographies.
www.HeroesThenAndNow.com